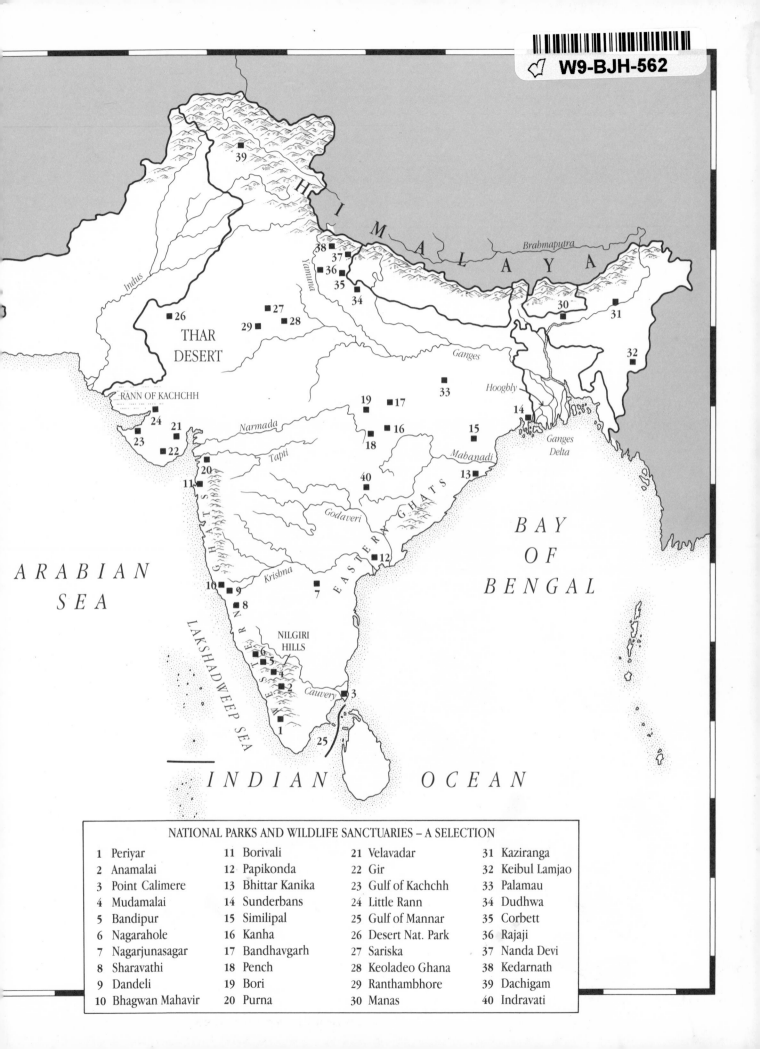

NATIONAL PARKS AND WILDLIFE SANCTUARIES – A SELECTION

1 Periyar	11 Borivali	21 Velavadar	31 Kaziranga
2 Anamalai	12 Papikonda	22 Gir	32 Keibul Lamjao
3 Point Calimere	13 Bhittar Kanika	23 Gulf of Kachchh	33 Palamau
4 Mudamalai	14 Sunderbans	24 Little Rann	34 Dudhwa
5 Bandipur	15 Similipal	25 Gulf of Mannar	35 Corbett
6 Nagarahole	16 Kanha	26 Desert Nat. Park	36 Rajaji
7 Nagarjunasagar	17 Bandhavgarh	27 Sariska	37 Nanda Devi
8 Sharavathi	18 Pench	28 Keoladeo Ghana	38 Kedarnath
9 Dandeli	19 Bori	29 Ranthambhore	39 Dachigam
10 Bhagwan Mahavir	20 Purna	30 Manas	40 Indravati

IN SEARCH OF
WILD INDIA

IN SEARCH OF
WILD INDIA

CHARLIE PYE-SMITH

UBSPD
UBS Publishers' Distributors Ltd.
New Delhi Bombay Bangalore Madras Calcutta
Patna Kanpur London

First published in 1993
by UBS Publishers' Distributors Ltd.
5, Ansari Road, New Delhi–110 002
in association with Boxtree Limited.

© North/South Productions 1992
Text © Charlie Pye-Smith 1992
Map © Raymond Turvey 1992
Designed by Kit Johnson

Typeset by Cambrian Typesetters, Frimley, Surrey
Printed and bound in Hong Kong

1 3 5 7 9 10 8 6 4 2

for Boxtree Limited
21 Broadwall
London SE1 9PL

A CIP catalogue record for this book is available from the
British Library.

ISBN 81–85674–56–6

In Search of Wild India is a companion book to 'Wild India',
a major Channel Four television series produced by North-
South Productions, in association with Bedi Films and
Nigel Ashcroft Associates, and in co-production with the
Discovery Channel and International Television
Enterprises Ltd (ITEL).

CONTENTS

Introduction

◆

A CAUTIONARY
TALE

The shoreline along the south coast of the Gulf of Kachchh is unusually bleak by
Indian standards: Gujarat's arid and monotonously flat hinterland – in places cultivated,
elsewhere left as scrub – runs straight into the ocean without the intervening blessing of
palm trees, thatched huts or flowering shrubs. Dotted along the coast are dozens of fishing
villages, one of the more substantial, with a population approaching 20,000, being Salaya.
It is by no means a pretty place, though it has an energetic and expansive feel about it.
The dusty lanes which run down to the seafront are home to a promiscuous gathering of
goats, dogs, fishermen and children. There is a decent harbour for trawlers and lesser craft,
and beside it an impressive boatyard. At the time of my first visit five wooden vessels,
each the size of a large warehouse, were under construction. There was none of the
infrastructure – cranes, sheds, dry docks – which one normally associates with such
activity: here the cavernous cargo boats seemed to rise from the oily sand like a
reconstituted teak forest. They were all built to the same specifications, each accounting for
ten months' work by forty men, and capable, once afloat, of transporting 1,000 sheep or
goats to Saudi Arabia for the annual *hadj*, the pilgrimage to Mecca.

Nowadays Salaya's boat-builders get most of their teak from
Africa and elsewhere.

7

I had come to Salaya with Rishad Pravez, a biologist who had spent five years studying the wildlife along the coast, and we began our search for some of his fishermen friends among the flat-roofed godowns behind the harbour. We were hoping to hire a trawler to take us out to the Gulf's coral reefs. In the freezers there were boxes of squid, mullet and pomfret; there were a few skate and tuna too, though we did not see any prawns, the "pink gold" of the surrounding seas. Eventually, we tracked down the fishermen in their living quarters some way back from the shore.

For much of the afternoon we sat in a courtyard with the head of the family. He was the eldest of six brothers, a wiry, fit-looking man of sixty with a complexion as weathered as driftwood. At one time, he explained, he and his family had been very poor, but luck and hard work had pulled them out of poverty and he was now a man of substance. The family owned eleven trawlers, and although the only ostentatious show of wealth was that of the gold rings and bangles worn by the wives, daughters and other brightly dressed females of the entourage, the brothers evidently made a fine living from fishing. Last year, said one of them, as though to confirm their prosperity, some of the women had flown from Bombay to Mecca for the *hadj*. Compared to most of the fishermen along the coast this family was immensely rich. Outside the compound the manifestations of poverty were all too obvious: in the thin-limbed, stunted bodies of the children; in the idiot offspring of inbred families; in the unsanitary conditions of the hovels where many were forced to live. And yet the rich and poor had much in common; they were hospitable to outsiders in the best tradition of Islam; and they were ill-educated and frighteningly fecund. Male literacy along the Gulf of Kachchh stood at 2–3 per cent; and illiteracy among women was said to be universal. Before we left the compound, the head of the family explained with considerable pride that he and his wife had had nine children, and that they now had somewhere in the region of eighty grandchildren, ten or more of whom already had children of their own. I was reminded of God's command to Adam in Genesis: "Go forth and multiply and subdue the earth." This family, like many along the coast, was doing precisely that. The Gulf's population was increasing at an alarming rate – average family size stood at around ten – and the marine environment was beginning to suffer from the inevitable plunder.

In the evening we talked to some of the men building the large cargo boats. In the old days – this is an ancient industry – the teak had come from India's own forests, but these had been so seriously depleted that the boat-builders were now forced to seek their raw materials elsewhere: teak from Africa and other hardwoods from Malaysia. Closer to home it was the Gulf's mangrove swamps which were suffering from human depredation. At one time mangrove forests stretched, virtually uninterrupted, along the whole length of the Gulf's south coast. Now the only thriving mangrove forests are to be found around the islands offshore. Despite the fact that these fall within a marine national park, and are supposedly protected, the mangroves are fast disappearing and the gulf's fishermen pay little heed to their conservation status. Rishad's team of scientists from Saurashtra University estimated that the fishing communities in Salaya and four neighbouring villages cut some 12,000 tons of mangrove each year. The leaves are used for camel fodder, large trunks for boat building, and smaller branches for fishing poles and firewood. At this rate of destruction, there will be no mangroves left in ten years' time.

*Forests are being felled even in the remotest corners of India; a
match factory in Port Blair, South Andaman island*

Many of the trawler owners could well afford to buy bottled gas with which to cook, yet they clung to the tradition of a wood fire, and outside every dwelling, however grand or mean, we saw stacks of chopped mangrove. "One of the saddest things," said a biologist I met later, "is that the fishermen just don't seem to have any concept of the damage they're doing. Perhaps some of the the old men do; but the young don't – ignorance is terribly destructive." By cutting the mangroves, the fishermen are doing a gross disservice to both themselves and future generations: mangrove swamps act as nurseries for the prawn fisheries, and once they have gone these fisheries will inevitably go into a decline. The destruction of the mangroves has also led to a dramatic release of silt, which in places has smothered and killed the coral reef. This in turn has affected the productivity of the Gulf and many forms of life – from fish to flamingoes – are likely to suffer as a result.

Pristine forest in West Bengal (opposite).

India is tremendously rich in birdlife, boasting over 900 resident species and a further 300 which overwinter here. The tailor bird is one of the many species which relies for its survival on the produce of India's forests (below).

Despite the ravages of past and present, the Gulf of Kachchh still boasts an astonishing wealth of wildlife. The only significant population of dugongs to be found between Arabia and Sri Lanka is present here; and the Gulf supports the best remaining coral reef on mainland India's west coast. It is also of outstanding importance for a great variety of waterbirds: India's only breeding populations of greater flamingo, lesser flamingo, white pelican and avocet nest here, and during the winter months vast numbers of

waders and wildfowl descend on the mudflats to roost and feed. Man's influence has been by no means entirely malign, and on the artificial saltings near Bedi Port, some thirty miles north of Salaya, we saw large flocks of flamingoes, sandpipers, godwits, plovers, dunlins, black-winged stilts and ruff. However, one cannot help reflecting that much of what one sees today – the flocks of waders, the raucous heronries, the lush mangroves and the multi-coloured coral – is unlikely to survive long into the next century. And what is happening in Salaya and elsewhere along the coast is also happening, perhaps more insidiously and at a gentler pace, throughout much of India: nature is in retreat, and it is not just India's wildlife which is suffering, but her human population too.

In India the relationship between people and nature is of such complexity that it makes no sense to consider one without the other: *In Search of Wild India* is an exploration of this tangled and tattered web of life. Outsiders tend to think of India as a nation of burgeoning cities; in a sense, it is, but over three-quarters of the population live in the countryside and make a living from the land – whether hunter-gatherers in the depths of the forests of Andra Pradesh, nomads travelling across the barren lands of Rajasthan, or wealthy cereal farmers in the Punjab, the health and prosperity (one talks in relative terms) of most rural Indians is inextricably tied up with the health of the natural world. To take just one example: virtually every Indian in the countryside depends to some extent on the products of forested land, whether to supply fodder for his livestock, fuelwood for cooking, or material with which to build dwellings and construct implements. Yet, all over India, forests are being destroyed, and people are suffering the consequences. As the forests retreat,

In many parts of the Indian sub-continent, the poor can no longer afford to burn their dead on a wood pyre (below left).

Forests provide the raw materials with which India's traditional fishermen fashion their boats and catamarans; a typical scene on a beach in Kerala (below right).

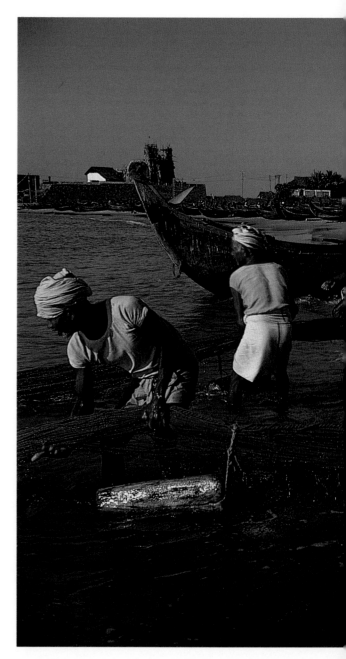

women must spend longer and longer searching for their daily firewood; and those who choose to buy it have seen prices spiral upwards, a reflection of both growing scarcity and increased demand. Traditional crafts are also affected by forest loss: in Tamil Nadu, fishermen are finding it hard to make their catamarans as the particular timber they require has become rarer and more expensive; in the villages of Karnataka, farmers can no longer afford to fit out their bullock

*The leopard has adapted to the human encroachment of its
habitat better than India's other large cats (overleaf).*

carts with wooden wheels. It is not just the living who suffer from the forest crisis, but the dead as well. In the Hindus' "eternal city" of Varanasi, the authorities have built an electric crematorium beside the River Ganges as the poor simply cannot afford to burn their dead on a cordwood pyre. Twenty years ago, 50 rupees or so would have purchased sufficient wood to burn a corpse; but the price of wood rose and people tried to economize, with gruesome consequences. Now it costs 800–1,000 rupees, or about a week's salary for a college lecturer, to cremate the dead on a wood pyre. This is far beyond the means of many Indians.

Such matters as these may seem parochial, especially when viewed in the context of climate change, or the increase in both floods and droughts – all of which can be attributed to deforestation – but they are illustrative of the close relationship between man and nature, whose respective fortunes and vicissitudes are inseparable. Over the past century, several species of animal have been driven to extinction in India, and others appear to be heading the same way. The disappearance of the Indian cheetah and the pink-headed duck is of little import as far as India's rural peasantry is concerned; but the same cannot be said of the disappearing forests and ebbing rivers. *In Search of Wild India* frequently has a sad tale to tell; but this book is as much a celebration as a dirge: a celebration of the astonishing variety of wildlife which India still supports, despite the best (or worst) efforts of Moghul hunters, British foresters and Indian industrialists; a celebration of some en-lightened conservation programmes; and, perhaps most significantly of all, a celebration of those individuals and organizations who are fighting, often against great odds and with little money, to save the natural world from further desecration.

Chapter One

◆

NATURE DEIFIED

Not long ago the graceful, swirling-horned Indian blackbuck – one of the loveliest of all the world's antelopes – was found across a broad swath of the Indian sub-continent. We can only guess at its past numbers, but some believe there may once have been as many as four million. The Emperor Akbar used to keep 1,000 cheetah with which to chase blackbuck, so there was certainly no scarcity in Moghul times. The conservationist M. K. Ranjitsinh, the leading authority on blackbuck, believes there were over 80,000 blackbuck in Saurashtra, in southern Gujarat, at the time of independence; by 1981, the same area held no more than 3,500. Across much of India this avid crop-raider, which was classified by the British as vermin, has been mercilessly persecuted. Ranjitsinh suggests that there are now around 40,000 blackbuck in the country; there would be many fewer had they not been revered and protected by the Bishnoi people of western Rajasthan and the Kathi of Gujarat.

Indian blackbuck once wandered across the sub-continent's grasslands in vast numbers. Persecution reduced their population from several million to 40,000 today; they are still plentiful around Bishnoi villages in Rajasthan, where they are revered and protected.

In many Indian paintings blackbuck graze fearlessly in the presence of men and maidens. A Moghul miniature from the eighteenth century.

At first glance there was nothing particularly remarkable about the countryside around Jodhpur, the largest city in western Rajasthan. A good chunk of it had been devoured by stone quarries and the rest was devoted to scrubby farmland: fields lay fallow in anticipation of the summer rains and elsewhere the hard ground was clothed with a smattering of thorn bushes and cacti. We pulled into the side of the road and switched off the car engine. Within minutes a landscape which had seemed unattractively drab was illuminated by brilliant splashes of moving colour. Two young Bishnoi women, dressed in dazzling reds and purples, swayed across a field, bundles of firewood balanced on their heads; a peacock strutted out from behind a bush and trailed long feathers of iridescent green and blue across the parched earth. A few minutes later a pair of blackbuck came into the field beside us, to be joined soon after by a large male nilgai, or blue bull, and a couple of chinkara gazelles. I was reminded of the Rajput and Moghul miniatures in which animals graze fearlessly in the company of men; thanks to the Bishnoi, such scenes of prelapsarian innocence can still be seen today.

Some 20 miles from Jodhpur, in the heart of Bishnoi country, the Forest Department has set up a small wildlife sanctuary. It consists of a large depression, a tenth of which was filled with water at the time of our visit, and a few acres of land surrounding it. We arrived in mid-morning to find half a dozen blackbuck feeding on the far side of the lake: more would come, suggested the watchman, Kolaram Bishnoi, once the gang of women who were chopping firewood left the waterside. A month earlier the lake had supported a large flock of migrating geese. These had gone now, but there were still plenty of other waterbirds: avocets, shellduck, gadwall, tufted duck, grey heron . . . I asked Kolaram about his people. He twirled his moustache and adjusted his turban: "About 500 years ago," he began, "a man called Jhambheji – a member of the Kshatriya, the warrior caste – was born near Bikaner. He became a saint and he had many followers. One of his teachings was that we should never allow anyone to kill blackbuck or chinkara or other deer." What would happen, I asked, if someone were imprudent enough to hunt these animals here? "Oh, we'd kill them," replied Kolaram in a very matter-of-fact way. "If a Bhil or a

Mahatma Gandhi described cow protection as "the central fact of Hinduism". Cows are revered by many and loathed by some. They provide power, transport, dung, hides and dairy products; they also clog up city traffic and overgraze much of India's forested land.

Nature worship is as ancient as man himself, and many Hindu beliefs borrowed heavily from the earthy cults of earlier times; an animist shrine in remote Ladakh.

Rajput came to hunt here we'd kill them. In fact a hunter did come recently. The villagers captured his jeep, burnt it and gave him a good beating. They nearly killed him." He pointed beyond the sanctuary. "In that village over there."

We do not know when blackbuck were first venerated. They appear in rock paintings in central India dating from 5000 BC and on seals of the Indus Valley civilization two millennia later. Following the Aryan invasion of 1500 BC and the emergence of Hinduism, blackbuck featured prominently in religious myths and fables. Nature worship is as ancient as man himself, and many of the animist beliefs which held sway among India's tribal peoples were later incorporated into the main body of Hindu mythology.

Hinduism is India's dominant religion, counting among its practitioners some four fifths of the population. To an outsider it appears an exotic, sensual, exuberant and often confusing religion. Mahatma Gandhi once called cow protection "the central fact of Hinduism", it being the one practice which united all Hindus. Hinduism differs from the other religions of India – Buddhism, Christianity, Islam, Jainism, Zoroastrianism – in that it has no single founder. Neither does it have a holy book, an equivalent to the Bible or the Koran; rather, Hindus find spiritual guidance in a variety of texts, especially the ancient *Vedas* (1600–1000 BC), the *Upanishads* (800–400 BC), the epic poetry of the *Mahabharata* and the *Ramayana*, and the *Puranas*. Hinduism is in many ways the most liberal of religions: Hindus can pick and choose which gods they wish to worship, which festivals and rituals they wish to observe. And yet it has a repressive side, exemplified by its rigid caste system and, in recent years, by the rise of Hindu fundamentalism, which makes a virtue of intolerance.

A Hindu shrine at the foot of a banyan tree; Goa (below).

Floral offerings in the Ganges at Varanasi (opposite).

There are many Hindus who live by the doctrine of *ahisma*, or non-violence, and they will go out of their way to cause no harm to living creatures; but there are others who place great emphasis on animal sacrifice. Contradictions such as these are accepted by Hindus with equanimity, just as the passage of sacred cows along the traffic-infested streets of Calcutta and Delhi raises no eyebrows.

During the months I spent in India I visited many holy sites – temples, shrines, mountain tops, rivers –

and reflecting on these journeys now, it is as though I am observing Hinduism through a kaleidoscope. At every glance the patterns seem to change: a multiplicity of gods and idols swim in and out of focus; rituals oscillate between the cerebral and the earthy. Naked *sadhus*, holy men who have renounced the material life, plunge into the icy head-waters of the Ganges; young women make offerings of flowers to a stone lingam, the phallic representation of Shiva; bus drivers sling a garland of orange marigolds round a photograph of Ganesh; and a million others worship in their own idiosyncratic ways. Nevertheless, Hinduism does have some unifying themes. Most importantly, all Hindus believe that humans pass through a cycle of rebirths, or reincarnations, which will eventually take them to *moksha*. Progress towards this point of spiritual salvation may be forward or backward, depending on your *karma*; evil deeds amount to bad *karma* and thus to a step down the ladder, while a virtuous life will take you nearer to *moksha*, the higher plane. In its passage towards *moksha* the soul travels, or transmigrates, between various forms, human, animal and spiritual; thus man's passage through life is intimately tied up with the animal world.

There is a marvellous sense of theatre about the vulture temple at Tirukkalikundram, a village some 40 miles south-west of Madras. I came here one scorching Sunday in April and made my way barefoot, in the company of several hundred others, up the 600 stone steps which led from the dusty village to the Shiva temple at the summit of a conical hill. The views were stupendous: the ragged streets below were dominated by two pairs of wedge-shaped stone temples, each encompassing slime-green tanks; beyond lay a parched landscape occasionally illuminated by a chink of emerald paddy.

In some parts of India, peafowl have become agricultural pests.
However, their sanctity has been their saving: the peacock is one
of the many sacred creatures in the Hindu pantheon.

The hill-top temple was modern: garishly poly-chromed outside, like an ice cream parlour, and gloomy inside. Off to one side a soft-drinks seller did swift business, while beyond, on a large rock, sat a dark-skinned priest, clothed only in a white *lungi* and sheltered from the piercing rays of the sun by a black umbrella. Beside the priest was a copper bowl which carried the meat with which he intended to tempt two vultures which were said to appear precisely at noon every day.

Noon came and went and the crowd swelled. Passing kites floated up on eddies of hot air and were greeted with screams of delight and encouragement. An hour passed, and still no vultures. A young man in western clothes suddenly stepped out of the crowd, unfurled a banana leaf, set some oil alight, singed the beard of a coconut, smashed it, dabbed sandal-paste on his forehead, offered frenetic prayers skywards, plunged to his belly, kissed the earth, then rose to scatter fragments of smashed coconut among the crowd. All this was observed with a mixture of mirth and reverence. Eventually, well into mid-afternoon, the vultures plummeted out of the sky, grabbed the meat and disappeared. The priest rose; the crowd dispersed; ritual was satisfied.

The vulture is one of dozens of creatures which populate the Hindu pantheon; some are seen as the mounts of gods and goddesses, some as their messengers, and some as reincarnations. The swan has been portrayed as a mount of both Brahma, the creator, and Saraswati, the goddess of knowledge; the peacock of Kartikeya; the eagle of Vishnu, the preserver; and the owl of Lakshmi, the goddess of wealth. In some parts of southern India, the Brahminy kite, the ever-present scavenger of slums and cities, is seen as a symbol of the goddess Durga, whose mount is the Asiatic lion. The rat is the incongruously small

mount of Ganesh, the elephant-headed god of wisdom and prosperity and a great favourite among Hindus: there is a temple in Rajasthan whose thriving population of rats is venerated and fed by the local people, and one of the more unnerving sights in Calcutta is the population of rats, perhaps 1,000-strong, which occupies a small triangle of much-burrowed parkland not far from the neo-classical town hall. I met one European, overwhelmed by the poverty of the city, who summed up his feelings thus: "Half the city's hungry, but people still come to

The peacock is a favourite subject in religious art, and frequently enlivens the façades of secular buildings too. This one is above the main entrance to Bombay's Victoria Terminus, a flamboyant example of tropical Gothic architecture.

The rat is the incongruously small mount of Ganesh, the elephant-headed god of wisdom and prosperity; these rats are given free board and lodging at a Hindu temple in Rajasthan (below).

Elephants, ceremonial parasols and traditional music combine to brilliant effect at the annual Pooram *festival at Trichur, Kerala (opposite).*

feed these rats!" The hungry themselves, more *au fait* with the mysteries of reincarnation than the foreign traveller, probably see nothing either anomalous or distasteful about the presence in their midst of this well-fed tribe of rodents.

Langurs, which owe their popularity to Hanuman, the monkey god who helped Rama to vanquish one of his enemies, are a familiar sight at many Hindu temples, but the noblest of all the temple animals is the elephant, which served in mythology as a mount for Indra, the god of rain and thunder. In southern India, elephants frequently take part in religious festivals, one of the most famous being the Trichur

Pooram in Kerala, when thirty magnificently clad males with gleaming tusks are gathered before the Vadakkunathan temple. Carvings of elephants adorn the walls of thousands of temples in India, and stone statues of the tusked beasts frequently guard the entries to shrines. Elephants also loom large in the immense rock bas-relief dedicated to the Shivite myth in Mahabalipuram, a town on the Tamil Nadu coast not far from Tirukkalikundram. The bas-relief, some 80 foot long by 20 high, was carved by Pallava craftsmen during the 7th and 8th centuries AD, and it tells the story of how Shiva broke the fall of the holy River Ganges as the waters tumbled from heaven to

*The magnificent rock bas-relief dedicated to the Shivite myth
in Mahabalipuram.*

An elephant blesses a Hindu pilgrim in the south Indian town of Madurai.

earth. For a thousand years Bhagiratha, a holy man, had lived a life of austerity – here, he is depicted standing on one leg – in order to encourage the gods to let the heavenly Ganges flow down to earth. When his wish was fulfilled there were fears lest the rushing waters destroy the earth, and Shiva generously agreed to take the force of water on his head. Observing this miracle are scores of exquisitely carved figures of gods, men and animals. The whole thing is dominated by two large elephants which face past the king and queen of the Nagas – the snake gods with serpentine tails and many-hooded heads – towards the frail figure of Bhagiratha. Other Hindu myths are depicted on smaller reliefs nearby. Especially lovely are the pastoral scenes – they might have been taken from today's countryside – telling the story of Krishna's life: here is the cowherd playing his flute; here is his wife bringing rice and buttermilk to the field; and here are Krishna's *gopis* with their enticing breasts and sensuous smiles.

For some creatures their sanctity has been their saving. To most Hindus the deliberate killing of a cow is almost as heinous a crime as the dispatching of a Brahmin; even the accidental slaughter of a cow requires the most elaborate of purification ceremonies. Likewise, in areas where the Brahminy kite is seen as a symbol of the goddess Durga, anybody who accidentally kills one of the birds must cremate it in a ceremony little different from the one more commonly reserved for humans. "Religion and superstition have caused the overpreservation of some animals and almost the extinction of others," wrote one disgruntled British naturalist earlier this century. The Hindus, he complained, did nothing to control the numbers of nilgai, blue pigeon, peafowl and monkey, all of which raided crops and depressed agricultural yields; at the same time the alleged medicinal

properties of rhinoceros horn had led to those animals being virtually wiped out. Hindu belief sometimes requires not just restraint from killing but active conservation, and in the past Indian peasants frequently found themselves in conflict with British hunters unwilling to respect their sensibilities. For example, in 1900, villagers chased four British soldiers, whom they observed shooting blue pigeons and peafowl near Umballa. One of the villagers was shot, while four others were tied up and beaten.

However, deification has not always been proof against persecution. The turtle, for example, is considered to be the ninth incarnation of Vishnu (who has also appeared as a boar, as a fish, as Krishna, as Buddha, and as the present king of Nepal), yet the olive Ridley turtles which come to nest on the shores of east India in January and February are shown little respect by many villagers: their eggs are dug up as a source of protein (they are cheaper than hens' eggs) and around the town of Tuticoran captured turtles are suspended from trees, split open with a knife and bled to death – drinking their blood is said to give relief to sufferers of piles and asthma. In the marshes to the east of Calcutta, freshwater turtles meet a similarly gory end. Passing through the small fish market at Bantana early one morning we saw a dozen small turtles lying on their backs, their legs waving helplessly in the air. Meat is scooped out of the live animals with a sharp knife: this way the buyer can be sure that the meat is fresh and the vendor gets a higher price than if they were dead. In Hindu mythology the crocodile acts as a vehicle for the deified River Ganges, but this has done nothing to help India's three species – the gharial, the mugger and the saltwater crocodile – all of which have been persecuted until recent times. Crocodiles, of course, do pose a threat to villagers sharing their watery habitat, so it is scarcely surprising if they are viewed with animosity; and the same, perhaps, can be said of snakes, which are said to kill more than 10,000 Indians each year.

Over the past few years environmentalists have become deeply concerned about the damming of the River Narmada, which flows westward across the rugged Deccan Peninsula to enter the Arabian Sea some way north of Bombay. There are many objections to this World Bank-financed scheme (they are fully aired in Chapter 7) but one which virtually every foreign journalist gets into his or her opening paragraph concerns the river's perceived sanctity. "Mother India's most sacred river is to be sacrificed," raged the *National Geographic*, while *The Times* saw things in terms of a "conflict between practical bureaucracy and emotional spirituality". Before I made my way down to the banks of the river I visited some prominent anti-dam campaigners in the town of Indore. They ran through their grievances: hundreds of thousands of people would be displaced by the dam and irrigation works; tens of thousands of acres

of virgin forest would be submerged; those who had the temerity to oppose the dam were being brutally dealt with by the authorities in Madhya Pradesh and Gujarat. And what about the river's sacredness, I asked? Wasn't the temple-studded Narmada considered to be even holier than the Ganges? The question was answered by Rahul Bartuti, a retired journalist and charismatic raconteur: "That's not really an issue," he suggested. "Western newspapers make much of the Holy Narmada, but they're just reflecting a western prejudice – the idea of India as the land of holy rivers and *sadhus*. Of course, we all have a sentimental attachment to the river, but religion simply is not an issue as far as most anti-dam campaigners are concerned. What people are talking about is the right to life – a right being denied all those whose homes and land will be flooded."

So wasn't the Narmada holy? "Yes," he replied, "but all rivers are holy, even those which have disappeared or been polluted. And in just the same way many mountain tops and woods are considered holy." Over several thousand years people had declared various parts of the landscape sacred. This was partly out of gratitude, according to Mr Bartuti: "Rivers sustain the world," he declared, "and without them we couldn't survive"; but he also saw this as an early example of conservation: "By making a mountain or wood sacred, it ensured that it wouldn't be defiled, that its trees wouldn't be chopped down." In verdant Kerala, the state of spice estates and waving palms, some of the best lowland forest is to be found in 70-odd sacred groves, which vary in size from 50 acres down to less than an acre. Further north, the states of Maharashtra and Goa have over 400 sacred groves, and these and many other wild places in India have only survived because of their religious associations.

Banyan trees are sacred to Hindus and Buddhists. This superb specimen is found behind the hunting lodge in Ranthambhore national park.

According to one of the *Puranas*, the Narmada is the holiest of India's rivers; just contemplating its waters is supposed to ensure eternal bliss, and even the Ganges is said to visit the Narmada once a year, in the guise of a black cow, in order to cleanse herself. However, the Ganges valley is the cradle of Indian civilization, and Ganga herself has a spiritual significance which cannot be exaggerated. She was, after all, the gift of the gods to a barren earth, and she has always inspired wonder and devotion.

Every year vast numbers of Hindu pilgrims, from well-to-do city businessmen to peasants and ash-smeared, tangle-haired, trident-carrying *sadhus*, make their way to the Ganges by air, road and foot. Some climb to the river's glacial source above Gangotri, 13,000 feet up in the Garhwal Himalaya; others make their way to the ashrams at Hardwar and Rishikesh; but the greatest number come to Varanasi, formerly Benares, whose river bank at dawn presents a spectacle of incomparable beauty. As the rising sun

A scene of incomparable beauty; every morning thousands of pilgrims descend on the ghats at Varanasi to bathe in Mother Ganga's holy waters.

casts a burnished glaze over the temples and ghats, a multitude of pilgrims descends on the river to bathe, to drink the holy waters, and sometimes to prepare for death. Soon after dawn wisps of smoke begin to rise from the funeral pyres at Harishchandran Ghat and midge-like clouds of swifts and house martins leave their mud nests in the back-alley eaves to wheel above the river in search of insects.

Sometime around the end of the 6th century BC a member of the Kshatriya caste journeyed from his home at Lumbini, near the present India–Nepal border, to a point on the Ganges 150 miles east of Varanasi. After a long spiritual struggle, lasting six years or more, Siddhartha Gautama decided to meditate beneath a pipal tree until he received enlightenment. It came after forty-nine days and Siddhartha – hence to be known as Buddha, the enlightened one – made his way to the Deer Park at Sarnath, a village a few miles from Varanasi, to preach his first sermon. Though there are only a few million Buddhists in India today, the preachings of their founder have been of profound significance to the nation's spiritual development. Buddha rejected the hierarchical Hindu caste system, which worked so powerfully in favour of the Brahmins, the priest caste, and he also deplored the practice of animal sacrifice. He taught his followers (and apparently even the deer listened at Sarnath) that there are four "noble truths": life is full of suffering; suffering is caused by desire; suffering can be overcome; suffering will cease if one follows the "Middle Way". Buddha warned against a life of extremes, spiritual or material, and he preached reverence for all forms of life.

Today Sarnath has been stripped of romance: the Deer Park does have some deer, but they are caged in scruffy enclosures, and one's passage around the complex of stupas and monastic ruins is constantly

Scenes from Buddha's life adorn the intricately carved gateway to the stupa at Sanchi near the town of Bhopal in Madhya Pradesh (below). The stupa was begun by Emperor Ashoka.

In Ashoka's day the Asiatic lion was found across a vast area stretching from Turkey to the Bay of Bengal. Now just a few hundred survive in Gujarat's Gir forest (opposite).

interrupted by hawkers and beggars. Nevertheless, Sarnath is worth visiting, if only to see the magnificent lion capital which once adorned a pillar erected here by Emperor Ashoka, who came to power around the year 273 BC.

Eight years into his rule Ashoka led an attack upon the region of Kalinga, which encompassed the Eastern Ghats between the rivers Godaveri and Mahanadi. Over 100,000 people were killed and many more were captured; Ashoka, though victorious, was filled with remorse and from then on devoted his life to promoting Buddhism and its principles. He gave up hunting and became a vegetarian; he built hospitals, dug bathing tanks and drinking wells, and planted shade trees for travellers. He also issued scores of edicts, which were carved into rocks and pillars scattered across the empire. His Fifth Pillar Edict may well have been the first written law of conservation: Ashoka decreed that various animals such as bats, rhinoceroses, monkeys and tree squirrels were to be strictly preserved and that "forests must not be burned, either for mischief or to destroy living creatures".

The lion capital at Sarnath is an object of great beauty, carved out of brown sandstone and highly polished. Four lions, symbolizing the four corners of the earth and Buddha's spiritual pre-eminence, are supported by an abacus with four other carved creatures, an elephant, a horse, a bull and another lion. This capital is now the emblem of the Indian government. There is an obvious irony here. In Ashoka's day, and indeed until relatively recently, the Asiatic lion was found across a vast area stretching from Turkey to Bengal. By the early years of this century, hunting and persecution had reduced their number to twenty or less, all hemmed into a small area of scrubby forest in the south of Gujarat. That their population is now back to several hundred is cause for rejoicing (though not, perhaps, for the many villagers whose relatives have been eaten or maimed by lions in recent years), but I am more inclined to think of the story of the Asiatic lion in terms of a collective apostasy: the Ashokan ideals of reverence for life being renounced in favour of a materialistic creed quite capable of justifying violence towards both man and nature.

Devout Buddhist though he was, Ashoka did not attempt to impose his religious beliefs on his subjects by any means other than gentle persuasion and good example. Admittedly, he forbade blood sacrifices, but the hunting of edible creatures (apart from those protected by his edicts) was still allowed, and he made no attempt to prevent his subjects from eating meat. Though most Buddhists and many high-caste Hindus were vegetarians, neither religion went as far as Jainism in attributing sanctity to all living things.

The Jain religion was founded by Mahavira, a contemporary of Buddha born near the Ganges in what is now Bihar. According to Jain belief, Mahavira – or "Great Spirit" – was the twenty-fourth and last of the Tirthankaras, which means "the ones

*Mount Abu in southern Rajasthan boasts some of the finest
examples of Jain architecture in India; this is the carved interior
of one of the Dilwara temples.*

who lead to the other shore". The other shore is the equivalent of the Hindus' *moksha*, but there are important doctrinal differences between Hinduism and Jainism. Like Buddha, Mahavira was opposed to the Hindu caste system and animal sacrifice. The central tenet of Jainism is *ahisma*, or non-violence, and if the soul is to eventually rid itself of bad *karma* and cross to the "other shore", all living things, no matter how humble, must be treated with reverence. Mahavira took asceticism, the hallmark of the Jain religion, to its logical conclusion: he starved himself to death at the age of seventy-two. All Jains are strict vegetarians, and one sect known as the Digambaras, or the "sky-clad", has even renounced the wearing of clothes (Alexander the Great called them the "naked philosophers"). Many Jain monks wear masks across their face to prevent them from inadvertently swallowing insects, and they sweep the ground before them with a small brush to ensure that they harm no life, however minuscule.

There are some 3.5 million Jains in India today, the majority living in the same state as the remnant population of Asiatic lions, whose forest homeland is overlooked by Girnar, one of the five hills considered sacred by these exemplary champions of *ahisma*. One does not expect a religion which puts such strong emphasis on self-denial (or, for that matter, one which denies the existence of a supreme Creator) to produce a lush, exuberant architecture. Yet that is precisely what the Jains have done.

The holiest of the hills held sacred by the Jains is Shatrunjaya, some 40 miles as the crow flies to the east of the Gir lion sanctuary. The approach is dull: cultivated fields, patches of scrubby acacia, a general drabness. Occasionally one passes yellow-turbaned peasants and haughty camels pulling carts; egrets and red-wattled plovers search ditches and village ponds

Indians have a passionate love of flowers. Lotus, marigold and several others play a colourful part in religious ceremonies, and women frequently wear garlands of heavy-scented jasmine in their lustrous hair. A garland seller in a Goan market.

for food; from time to time a haphazard collection of golden orioles, Kashmiri rollers and rose-ringed parakeets gives the telegraph wires the appearance of an exotic musical score. But the real drama begins at the foot of Shatrunjaya. For over nine hundred years, pilgrims have climbed up this steep hill to the marble temples on its summit. By the time I arrived, an hour or so after dawn one hot September morning, hundreds had already reached the temples; thousands more would follow during the course of the day. The old and infirm were carried up the 5,000 or so steps in two-man litters, or *dolis*; the rest walked to the top, halting occasionally to draw breath and observe the shimmering views across the plains below. Shatrunjaya means "place of victory over worldliness" and the whole complex of marble temples – 863 in all – feels gloriously celestial.

Victory over worldliness is one thing; victory over nature quite another. All too often nowadays man talks in terms of the conquest of nature, as though nature were an enemy to be subdued. Hinduism, Buddhism, Jainism – each has its own particular, and sometimes peculiar, way of looking at the natural world, but nowhere, in all their diverse teachings, do they sanction the many abuses of nature which have now become commonplace, even in this most holy of nations. On one of my last visits to India I stood early one morning on a river bank beside Bombay's Mahim Creek. Slum-dwellers performed their ablutions beside the oily waters which lapped around the stunted mangroves. Beyond lay the sprawl of Dharavi, which is said to be the largest slum in Asia, and in the far distance the angular skyline of downtown Bombay cut through the early morning haze. Every half-minute or so a train clattered across an iron bridge which spanned the creek, carrying commuters towards the city and their work. As each

train crossed the bridge carrier bags were hurled from the doors and windows into the waters below. Before long the piers of the bridge were garlanded with white plastic and other assorted waste. It struck me as a senseless way to dispose of rubbish and I said so to my companion. "Ah, you don't understand," he exclaimed with a grin. "That's not rubbish they're throwing away – it's the marigolds and other temple flowers which they used at home. You see, they can't just put them in their rubbish bins; belief decrees that these sacred flowers should be delivered to a river or into the sea." It was sad to see this beautiful custom debased by tawdry packaging. This was a small thing, perhaps, but it seemed to capture the flavour of modern India: the sacred and the profane are never far apart.

Chapter Two

NATURE TAMED

When the first Aryans arrived from Iran some time around 1500 BC, they found in the
Indus Valley a sophisticated civilization, although it was already in decline, its cities
partially wrecked by floods, its agricultural land gradually turning to desert. The Aryans
defeated and enslaved the darker-skinned natives and before long their influence spread
across northern India. "Their onslaught was like a hurricane," wrote one chronicler of the
day. Much the same could be said of the Moghul conquest in the sixteenth century AD.
During the intervening years India had experienced many invasions – of people, religions
and ideas – but none so dramatic as the one lead by Babur in 1526. Babur considered his
own kingdom of Ferghana inadequate for a man of his pretensions and background – he
was descended from the Emperor Timor and the notorious pillager Genghis Khan –
and he made repeated attempts to capture Samarkand. Although the city came under
his rule for brief spells, he was always driven out; so he turned his attentions
to India instead. He conquered the Muslim-controlled Delhi Sultanate in 1526 and the
Hindu forces marshalled under the Rajput leaders at Khanna the following year.

*Although the Moghuls were great nature lovers, they sought to
impose order on the world around them. The Taj Mahal, the
mausoleum built by Shah Jehan to house the body of his wife
Mumtaz, was the supreme architectural achievement of the
Moghul period. The Bengali poet Rabindranath Tagore
described it as "A tear in the face of eternity".*

Babur's initial attitudes towards the conquered land were ambivalent. "Hindustan is a country of few charms," he wrote in his *Memoirs*. "Its people have no good looks; of social intercourse, paying and receiving visits, there is none . . . there are no good horses, no good dogs, no grapes, musk-melons or first-rate fruits, no ice or cold water, no good bread or cooked food in the bazaars, no hot baths, no colleges, no candles, torches or candlesticks. . . . There is an excessive quantity of earth and dust flying about." Yet elsewhere in his *Memoirs* Babur enthused: "It is a wonderful country. Compared with our countries it is a different world; its land, its animals and plants, its peoples and their tongues, its rains and its winds, are all different."

Before the arrival of the Moghuls the Indian people lived somewhat anarchically within nature: cultivating land where crops thrived; clearing forests where it suited them; hunting animals for food or skins; living, in short, not as masters of nature, but as part of it. With the coming of the Moghuls, all this changed. Many of the emperors were great nature lovers, but they sought to impose some order, some symmetry, on the world around them.

Babur's initial disenchantment with India was said to be a reflection of its lack of verdant gardens, a defect he rapidly remedied by building some himself. Over the next century and a half, the Moghul rulers were to create scores of fine gardens throughout their empire, and it was they who introduced the idea of the "Paradise Garden". (Our word "paradise" comes from the Persian word *pairidaeza*, which means a walled garden.) Many of the great Moghul tombs – the Taj Mahal being the most celebrated – are to be found within such gardens, which were often designed to represent the Koranic heaven. A reverence for water, trees, flowers and order is always apparent. "As with the Persians, flowering trees represented renewal," wrote Elizabeth Moynihan in her study, *Paradise as a Garden*. "The cypress represented eternity to the Mughals and bordered the walks and waterchannels of their gardens. Orange and citron were also favoured for these borders; pomegranates, almonds and date palms were grouped in the plots. . . . Beneath the groves of trees, masses of spring-flowering plants – iris, daffodils and narcissus – were preferred . . . many hybridized roses were cultivated, and jasmine was a great favourite, especially in the strongly scented moonlight gardens." I imagine that it was from a garden such as this that Adam and Eve were expelled after committing the original sin, and indeed the following words are inscribed above the entrance to the tomb of Akbar, grandson of Babur and arguably the greatest Indian ruler since Ashoka: "These are the Gardens of Eden: enter them to dwell therein eternally."

The Moghuls today are best remembered for their architectural genius: Akbar for the magnificent royal city of Fatehpur Sikri and the Red Fort at Agra; Jahangir for his gardens, especially in Kashmir; and Shah Jehan for the Red Fort in Delhi and the Taj Mahal, which the Bengali poet Rabindranath Tagore described as "a tear in the face of eternity". Many of these fabulous buildings now seem devoid of life, though here and there nature intrudes, much as she must have done during the days of the Moghuls. Dashing flocks of rose-ringed parakeets, brilliant emerald against the rich purple of the sandstone, swoop around the battlements of Fatehpur Sikri, while swallows and martins feed in their thousands over the Taj and the Red Fort. But there was a time when the moat around the fort was more than just a resting-place for discarded sweet-wrappings and

*Moghul gardens, shaped by a reverence for water, trees, flowers
and order, were often conceived as a Koranic heaven on earth.
Their sublime quality can be seen here in a garden in
Srinagar, Kashmir.*

sated vultures; any enemy foolish enough to trespass here would have been greeted by tigers, leopards, crocodiles and other hostile creatures. And within the cities themselves the traveller would have encountered an exotic menagerie: cheetahs trained for the chasing of blackbuck and deer; falcons for the hunting of game birds; elephant from which to conduct both wars and hunts.

Akbar was never able to read or write, yet he was an intelligent and cultured man who did much to promote the arts. In his Moghul painting atelier, previously established by his father, Akbar employed 100 artists to work under two Persian masters. They ignored the Islamic injunction which forbade the portrayal of humans and animals, and Moghul miniatures were thus free to reveal much about the passions and preoccupations of the day, from courtly love to religious discourse, from ordered landscapes to the dramas of the hunt. The art of the Moghul miniature was most exquisitely practised during the rule of Jahangir, and the paintings tell of his deep love of the natural world. Jahangir was one of the great garden builders of Moghul times and these are depicted in many miniatures: the emperor walks beside a cypress-lined stream, a drongo flying overhead; maidens and deer consort beneath a canopy of fruit and flowering shrubs; squirrels chase each other up the sacred Chenar tree. In all the paintings of this period the impression is of nature tamed; nature, in the Moghul scheme of things, was intended to serve, not thwart.

The Muslim citadel of Bijapur etched against a fiery
dusk (opposite).

A lone kite patrols the roofs of Akbar's royal city, Fatehpur
Sikri (below).

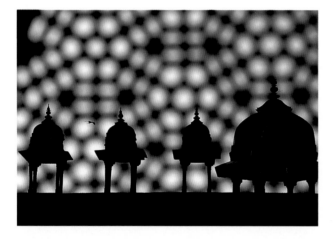

The writings of Babur and Jahangir are illuminated
by their love of nature; even after a wearying battle,
the former took time to note down the unfamiliar
birds and flowers he had seen, and Jahangir's
memoirs read like a nature diary. Both the emperors
were passionate about hunting too, and under the
Moghuls the organized slaying of animals was
conducted on a scale seldom witnessed before or
since. Jahangir kept meticulous records of his hunting
escapades, which show that between 1580 and 1616
28,532 animals were killed in his presence, over half
by the emperor himself. His father Akbar also kept
accounts. When chasing the tiger, he favoured
sometimes the bow and arrow, sometimes the
shotgun; he was also fond of falconry and the setting
of cheetah and lynx after deer and other game.

The sheer scale of many hunts was astounding.
Akbar once employed 50,000 beaters for a hunt near
Lahore, and the last of the great Moghul emperors,
Aurangzeb, used whole armies to flush out game.
One of the most graphic descriptions of a hunt is
given by William Blane, an Englishman who attended
the hunting excursions of Asoph ul Doulah, a vizier

of the then-declining Moghul empire and Nawab of Oudh in the latter part of the 18th century. The nawab's hunting party used to set out in December every year and would stay out till March, covering some 400–600 miles. The nawab was accompanied by his court and household, "and a great part of the inhabitants of his capital". Beside his immediate attendants, who numbered around 2,000, he also had 500–600 horses, several battalions of sepoys and up to 500 elephants. As well as all this, recalled Blane, "there is a large public bazaar, or, in other words, a moving town attends his camp, consisting of shop-keepers and artificers of all kinds, money-changers, dancing women, etc." All in all, the party was 20,000-strong.

A great variety of arms were carried for the killing of animals – matchlocks, pistols, bows and arrows, swords, sabres, daggers – and the nawab was also accompanied by a variety of hunting beasts: "The animals he carries for sport are dogs, principally greyhounds, of which he has about 300 – hawks, of various kinds, at least 200; a few trained leopards – called *cheetahs* – for catching deer; and to this list I may add a great many marksmen, whose profession is to shoot deer; and fowlers who provide game. . . ." For entertainment, the nawab had fighting buffaloes, fighting rams, fighting cocks, pigeons, nightingales and parrots: all performers in his mobile zoo.

The nawab would rise before dawn, take a hot bath and English breakfast, then set out for the day's carnage. On a good day he would bag two or three tigers, even slaughtering females and cubs when encountered. Wild elephants, buffaloes and rhinoceroses were shot in large numbers; dogs were sent after foxes, jackals and deer; hawks were let fly at partridges, bustards, quails and herons; wild boar were either shot or hunted with dogs.

Of the six great Moghul emperors, the least attractive was the last, Aurangzeb: a fanatical Muslim, he alienated the country's Hindu population by reviving a tax on non-Muslims, and during his rule the arts suffered grievously. It is said that in order to fulfil what he saw as Islamic law, he personally knocked the jewelled heads off the bas-reliefs of lions, peacocks and other animals in Fatehpur Sikri; and he was as bigoted as Akbar, that great city's founder, had been enlightened. Aurangzeb expanded the empire's territory, but after his death in 1712 it swiftly began to fragment; the Deccan, from 1724, was ruled by its Muslim governor; the Hindu Marathas took control of a large region in the west; and Gujarat, Oudh and the Punjab went their own way in the 1750s.

The collapse of the Moghul system of government proved highly advantageous to the British. For over 150 years the East India Company, which had been granted a monopoly on British trade in India by a charter of 1600, had steadily extended its commercial tentacles across the sub-continent. In 1756 the Nawab of Bengal imprudently attacked Calcutta, a possession of the company, consigning some of the white inhabitants to the infamous "Black Hole". This led to the Battle of Plassey, at which the nawab and his French allies were defeated by Robert Clive's army. From then on the company's grip on the country tightened, and the process of colonization was to be completed following the Indian Mutiny of 1857, after which the East India Company was disbanded and the British Crown took over the running of the country. The British had come to India for reasons of commerce – at one time India was referred to as "a plantation" – and the impact they had on the country's landscape and wildlife was to be profound.

At one time the British referred to India as a "plantation" and
much of the country proved ideal for growing crops such as
tea, coffee, sugar, cotton and fast-growing timber like
eucalyptus. Tea gardens still dominate the Nilgiri landscape in
southern India.

Ootacamund (opposite) was established in the Nilgiris by the British in the early nineteenth century. Nowadays the old "queen of the hills" is plagued by squatter settlements, pollution and unfettered tourist development.

Symbols of progress: the elephant tamed and the arrival of steam on a bas-relief at Victoria Terminus, Bombay (below).

To catch the flavour of the Moghul period, you should drift through the palatial halls of Fatehpur Sikri, or wander round the Taj Mahal one shimmering dawn; to recall the British era, you should clamber on to an ancient steam train and chug through tea gardens and terraced farmland to one of the many hill stations built by the British between 1815 and 1947, the year of their departure.

Ootacamund – or "snooty Ooty", as it was once known – is one of the chief hill resorts of southern India, set in a rolling landscape some 6,000 feet up in the Nilgiri Hills. Ooty today is overcrowded, run-down and polluted – the sewage system, built by the British to serve 22,000 people, must now cope with the effluent of 164,000 – and those who have grown up in and around this part of the Nilgiris talk of their homeland in elegiac terms: paradise, for them, has recently been lost. For those like myself who know the Nilgiris only as they are now, they remain one of the loveliest areas in southern India. The leisurely climb, over a period of two days in early April, from the foetid and oppressive heat of Cochin on the Kerala coast to the cool heights of the northern Nilgiris was a memorable experience. In Cochin everyone was weighed down by a pre-monsoon lassitude: the fishermen working the bamboo-slung Chinese nets, the boatmen ferrying people out to Bolghatty Island, even the dolphins in the harbour's oily waters – all moved with exaggerated and exasperating slowness. To travel from such an enervating climate to the freshness of the Nilgiris was to understand why the British, during their rule of India, fled the coasts and plains during the summer months and headed for the temperate hills. Watching the change in vegetation, as rice paddies, coconut and cardamom gave way to tea and eucalyptus, I could imagine the relief and elation that must have been felt by the government officials of the Raj and their *mem-sahibs*, as they made their way, by horse and carriage and later by steam train, up the steep slopes to Ooty.

The resort they found was peaceful, decorous and clean – a far cry from the Ooty of today, whose surrounding hills are scarred with squatter encroachments and whose ruptured pavements are coated with a scum of litter and decaying organic matter. Many of the splendours inherited from the days of the Raj now seem distinctly shabby, although they still lend the town a certain charm. A hint of past grandeur – and a window on how the other hundredth lived – can be seen in Fernhill Palace, once the summer residence for the Maharajah of Mysore and now a dilapidated hotel. There is a large ballroom with an out-of-tune piano and heavy leather armchairs; sepia photos of very English hunting scenes – red coats and sherry on the lawn, though the quarry was jackal not fox – hang from peeling walls of long corridors; and there is an elegant games room with a tattered snooker table and broken cues. Not that everything in Ooty is suffering from neglect. The botanic gardens, established in 1847 by the Marquis of Tweedale, are beautifully kept (and a good place to observe the Nilgiris' bird-

life), and there are some very English villas with manicured lawns, neat beds of tea-roses and names like *Belle Vista*.

And *belle vistas* were everywhere to be had when the British first arrived. In the Nilgiri Wildlife Association's Centenary Report of 1977, H. L. Townsend described the old Nilgiris thus: "Imagine then this plateau, a spider's web of countless streams, converging ultimately to become dignified as rivers and falls of great beauty. A patchwork of swamps and marshes, rolling grasslands, with every fold and ravine clothed in evergreen woods or *sholas*, the whole abounding in a wide variety of wildlife both fur and feather. Such was this rare jewel of nature, guarded for so long from the foreign invader by the malarial forests of the foothills, at the beginning of what is known officially as the English Period. . . ."

Since time immemorial the Nilgiris had been home to the Todas, a tribal group who had evidently lived in peaceful coexistence with the creatures of forest and grassland. Some time around the fifteenth or sixteenth centuries, the Todas were joined by the Badagas, who were said to be profligate in their use of forest products, but whose influence on wildlife was relatively benign. It was only when the British arrived that the Nilgiris' fauna began to suffer. The first British explorers to penetrate the forests and climb on to the Nilgiris were a revenue surveyor and his assistant in 1812. Further expeditions followed and in 1821 several British families took up temporary residence. In 1822 the first house was built in Ooty, which, over the coming years, was to prosper as a sanatorium – hitherto, the sick in Madras had been dispatched to the South African Cape to recover – and as a summer seat of government for the Madras Presidency. Land was progressively cleared and settled, the climate proving perfect for the growing

*Steam trains helped the British to open up India's wildernesses
– and they also contributed to their destruction as large quantities
of timber were required for the building and running of the
railways. An evocative scene; steaming up to Darjeeling.*

of crops like tea, coffee and potatoes. Naturally, this taming of the wilderness had a profound effect on the vegetation, but it was relentless hunting which drove the larger mammals and many birds off the hills. According to Townsend, himself a hunter: "From this time on [the 1860s] game of all kinds was steadily killed off, shooting went on all the year round and everything in the shape of game whether winged or four-footed was ruthlessly slain without regard for age, sex or season. To add to the destruction meted out by the Europeans, a race of local shikaries [hunters] had grow up and a very lucrative business was established in the supply of meat, both to the market, and private employees."

In those days the British and Indian worlds seldom fused, either socially or architecturally, but hovering between the two today is a small and largely impoverished community of Anglo-Indians, many of whom meet daily for lunch in the Chinese restaurant near Higginbotham's bookshop, the men dressed in tweed jackets and cavalry twills, the women in summer frocks and cardigans. All this seems strange, though in reality it is no stranger than the landscape outside. "Stand anywhere in Ooty and look around you," suggested N. Mohanraj, the secretary of the Nilgiri Wildlife Association, "and no matter where you look, every tree, every flower, every blade of grass you see will be exotic, an import of the British."

The British saw their eastern colonies, of which India was by far the most important, as fruit ripe for the picking. They were urged by one magazine to "grow there sugar, rice, cotton, tea, indigo, encourage the silk-worm, and culture of tobacco, opium etc.". And that is precisely what they did. Across the country forest was cleared to make way for cash crops; in the Nilgiris the native *sholas* – the evergreen forests – were replaced by tea gardens and fast-growing trees like eucalyptus; elsewhere cotton, sugar and dozens of other crops opened up the landscape and turned the wild lands into profitable concerns. Forests were felled not just to make way for agricultural expansion but to satisfy the rapidly expanding timber requirements of Britain and her colonies, for the construction of houses, factories, ships, and of course for export. In order to facilitate trade and the movement of goods and people around the country, the British built thousands of miles of new road and an ambitious railway system, the construction and running of which required large quantities of raw materials, especially timber and fuel.

Places which previously had known only sylvan seclusion soon throbbed with activity; and what happened during the previous century to the Doon Valley, in the foothills of the Himalaya, happened over much of India. The British had arrived here in 1815, and a rough census suggested a population of around 17,000. Soon they had built roads and railways connecting the valley to the plains further south, drained marshes and swamps, cleared forest and scrub, established a system of canals to irrigate the new cropland, created an administrative capital in Dehra Dun and opened up a hill station at Mussourie. By 1881 the valley's population had risen to 99,000; by 1901 to 127,000. So much forest had been cleared that in 1886 one British official was moved to observe: "Perhaps no mistake was more common in the early days of British rule than to suppose that the extension of cultivation wherever culturable land could be found, and the clearing of forest and jungle to extend cultivation, must necessarily benefit the country and Government, and should be encouraged and pushed on as much as possible." This enlightened official went on to argue that the conservation of large areas of forest was vital, especially in tropical areas, but British forestry policy was the antithesis of good environmental sense. Forests were primarily managed – or mismanaged – to supply the nation with timber, and local people were often excluded from the forests on whose produce they had traditionally depended.

It is hard to say to what extent it was habitat clearance, and especially forest destruction, and to what extent it was hunting that led to the rapid decline in numbers of many mammals and birds. It was a mixture of the two, and in some areas and for some species, one factor was more important than the other. Hunting was a great passion of the British

The coconut provides food, shelter and an important source of income for many thousands of people living along the Indian coast (left).

Betel-nut palms were probably introduced to western India from Malaya many centuries ago. Today betel-nut is a significant cash crop in the states of Goa and Karnataka (below).

and it was done both for pleasure and, in the eyes of the hunters at least, as a necessity, as a way of ridding the country of man-eating tigers and crop-raiding herbivores.

Rewards were frequently offered for the killing of animals classified as "vermin", and these were highly efficacious in bringing about the extermination of elephant, tiger, blackbuck, leopard and many other creatures in certain areas. A district officer in Bengal wrote in 1878 that "the Government offers so high a reward for the destruction of tigers and leopards that a hundred skins have been brought to me by one party of hunters, who had been prowling around the country setting bows charged with poisoned arrows." He went on to say that one of the great advantages of British rule was that wild beasts had been wiped out in food-producing districts: "In parts of Bihar which, a century or two ago, were described as without a trace of cultivation, and

A familiar scene in nineteenth century India. Many of India's
large mammals were slaughtered to satisfy the colonial blood lust.
The royal Bengal tiger was one of the principal victims.

abandoned to tigers and wild boars, the tiger is now entitled to rank with the extinct cave-lion." Yet four decades later another British sportsman reported that villagers often thought the damage done to their herds of cattle by tigers was more than compensated for by the tigers keeping down the population of wild pigs, which were great crop-ravagers. "Forty years ago rhinoceros were extremely numerous," wrote the same sportsman, "and several might be killed in one day. Owing to indiscriminate slaughter of both sexes and all sizes, their numbers have been terribly reduced." This was in the north of India; meanwhile, down in the south, the elephant was likewise persecuted. Midway through the last century the Madras Presidency encouraged their slaughter by offering a bounty, and one Englishman was reported to have killed 300 of the beasts – around a fifth of the number which remain today in the elephant-rich belt of land to the north of the Nilgiris.

According to John MacKenzie's admirable study, *The Empire of Nature*, "The British in India fused two hunting traditions. They adapted some of the spectacular forms of the Mughal Empire and of its inheritor princely States, many of which were preserved after 1858. They also adopted the more humble practices of low-caste Indian hunters and in the course of the nineteenth century appropriated the words *shikar* (hunting) and *shikari* (hunter) from them. To these they added classic British activities like fox hunting, angling and a form of *battue*. . . ." They enthusiastically adopted the use of spear and knife, but they also applied the rapidly developing precision of nineteenth-century firearms. . . ."

Many British hunters believed that by ridding the countryside of tigers and other "vermin" they were doing villagers and farmers a favour. But most hunters were motivated not by altruism but by the excitement and diversion of the hunt. Old accounts emphasize the pleasures to be had in the sport, which well into this century was frequently conducted on a magnificent scale. For example, in 1911 George V visited Chitwan, just over the Nepalese border, where he was escorted by the ruling maharajah accompanied by 12,000 followers and retainers and 600 elephants. During his week in Chitwan, the king's party bagged 39 tigers, 12 rhinoceroses and 4 bears. Exactly fifty years later Queen Elizabeth and Prince Philip also visited Chitwan; much to his credit, Prince Philip arrived with a bandage on his trigger finger and declined to join the shoot. At lunch the Queen was offered twenty-two varieties of game, including the rare florican crane; she chose peafowl pilau. On the same trip the Queen and Prince visited Ranthambhore, the hunting grounds of the Maharajahs of Jaipur, and today one of India's most beautiful national parks. In the *art deco* hunting lodge at nearby Sawai Madhopur there is a photograph of the royal couple standing in the company of other dignitaries over the corpse of a large tiger.

Many of India's maharajahs, having recently fallen on hard times, have turned their palaces and hunting lodges into guest houses, thus allowing visitors a glimpse of their once opulent lifestyles. These delightful places are often decorated with photographs of hunting scenes – an especially memorable

one in Jaipur's Bissau Palace shows the maharajah with a "bag" of seventy-three wild boar – and with hunting trophies, one of the largest collections being at the Goldbagh Palace outside Keoladeo Ghana sanctuary at Bharatpur, where a couple of hundred heads stud the walls. Keoladeo Ghana is one of the world's finest bird sanctuaries and its curious history is discussed in Chapter 5; suffice it to say here that this wetland paradise is entirely man-made and was created in the nineteenth century by a maharajah to attract wildfowl. He was successful beyond his dreams, and over the years astonishing numbers of birds were shot – without, it seems, causing any decline in their number. In a shoot in December 1914 held for Lord Harding, 4,062 birds were shot by 49 guns; two years later 51 guns accounted for 4,206 birds; and in 1938 a record was set in the presence of Lord Linlithgow when 4,273 birds were bagged. Further north in Rajasthan, near the town of Bikaner, Viceroy Irwin went on a shoot in 1929 in which over 10,000 imperial sandgrouse were killed.

By this time some people were openly expressing concern about the impact that hunting was having on wildlife populations. A series of pamphlets published between 1936 and 1939 by the All India Conference for the Preservation of Wildlife, and edited by Major Jim Corbett, showed that the hunts and shoots organized by the maharajahs and British ruling élite probably accounted for only a small fraction of the animals slain each year. The pamphlets pointed to the inadequacies of the 1912 Wild Birds and Animals Protection Act, and they told of the "terrible damage being done by shooting over water". The killing of animals for profit was leading to the decline of many species. The Punjab alone was said to have 20,000 *shikaris*. Of the 16,000 partridge which were sold in Delhi markets during four months of 1938, almost

India's wildlife is put to some curious uses. Ayurvedic sex doctors in Old Delhi make a witches' brew of spiny lizards (below).

Nature tamed – Alexandrine parakeets in Calcutta's bird market (opposite).

three-quarters had been taken by five licensed nets-men from just one district in Punjab. At the same time the shooting in the Eastern Ghats of gaur and deer for their hides had so diminished their populations that tigers had been forced to prey on humans and cattle instead. Poaching was a perennial problem, affecting all manner of creature from elephant and rhinoceros to wild cats and blackbuck. As one correspondent put it: "How the fauna of the world is being exterminated to satisfy the greed of man and his wife!"

Flipping through these musty pamphlets today one is struck by the many advertisements aimed specifically at hunters. For example, in an early volume from 1936 there is a picture of thirteen stuffed tigers' heads, the handiwork of a Mr van Ingen, Artist in

Taxidermy, Mysore. In fact, there is nothing odd about this: most of India's pioneer conservationists first made their acquaintance with wildlife when staring down the barrel of a gun. Some of these great hunter-naturalists are still alive: Mr R. Radcliffe, a retired British coffee-planter living near Ooty, has for a long time been a leading figure in the Nilgiri Wildlife and Environment Association; at one time he was a keen hunter, especially of tiger, leopard and wild boar. "I have no twinges of conscience for what I have done and no shame in declaring it," he wrote in 1977. Likewise, two of the key members of the Friends of Doon – both now retired after distinguished careers in industry and the civil service – told me over a beer in Dehra Dun about the weeks they had spent hunting game in the years before and after independence.

The ultimate statement of colonial might, Calcutta's Victoria Memorial was seen by many as Britain's answer – and a poor one at that – to the Taj Mahal.

One had now become a vegetarian and was almost Jain-like in his views; but listening to his stories I felt that this progression from hunter to conservationist was perfectly natural. Undoubtedly the greatest hunter-naturalist of them all was Major Jim Corbett, whose many books describing his adventures tracking down man-eating tigers are still in print. Back in the 1930s Corbett warned that forest destruction and over-zealous hunting could one day render the tiger extinct. Few people took much notice; after all, the tiger population was then thought to be 40,000 or more. Sadly, Corbett's prediction came perilously close to being fulfilled; by the time the Indian government launched Project Tiger in 1972, there were fewer than 2,000 tigers left in India.

Independence, won in 1947, did not bring any relief for the tiger, or for that matter for any of India's wildlife; rather, the opposite was true. Under the British there had been some controls over hunting; these now fell by the wayside and virtually everyone who had a weapon took to the fields and forests. India was gripped by an orgy of killing which took years to bring under control. None of this was helped by the attitude of the government, which supplied farmers with guns to protect their crops, and animals like blackbuck were swiftly exterminated in many areas. The government, of course, had inherited a whole range of problems which British officialdom had largely ignored; many rural areas suffered dreadful poverty and parts of the country frequently experienced famine. One of the main priorities was to grow more food for the rapidly expanding population, so millions of acres of forest were felled to make way for crops, and thus, inadvertently, were sown the seeds of many of the country's environmental problems.

Chapter Three

♦

THE WILL TO CONSERVE

Dawn breaks with lightning speed in India. When we left the scruffy outskirts of Sawai Madhopur, a small town in southern Rajasthan, the sky was a star-spangled coal-black; ten minutes later, as we sped south towards the rugged hills of Ranthambhore national park, the stars faded and the sky rapidly turned from iodine-purple to blush-pink and the palest of blues. By the time we reached the lake below Ranthambhore fort, the first rays of the rising sun were squinting through the trees, throwing ethereal rods of light across the hanging mists. A white-breasted kingfisher sat as still as stone above the silent water, as though stunned by the dawning of a new day; a purple moorhen skulked among the reeds, while further out, in the lee of an island just large enough to hold a few trees and a small temple, a mugger crocodile glided slowly shorewards. Across the other side of the lake grazed a small herd of heavy-antlered sambar; behind us, where a patch of grassland faded into forest, a dozen spotted deer stood sniffing the cool air, their senses alert to the threat of leopard or tiger.

There were probably 40,000 tigers in India at the turn of the century. Seventy years later there were fewer than 2,000. Thanks to Project Tiger, their population has since doubled.

*Chital, or spotted deer, are common throughout most of India in
lightly forested areas.*

India has such a variety of dazzling landscapes that one is loath to profess a preference, but there is something special about Ranthambhore. This is partly a reflection of its ever-changing character. During the course of an hour or two you will travel through rolling grasslands, heavily wooded valleys and deep ravines with sheer cliffs and rushing streams; you will ford rivers, drive round placid lakes and pass through open scrub and groves of mango and pipal. The bird life is profuse and colourful: within the park's 150 square miles some 270 species have been recorded, rather more than are to be found in mainland Britain. Within half an hour we had seen pond heron, cattle egret, Kashmiri roller, black drongo, spotted owl, honey buzzard, blossom-headed parakeet, golden-backed woodpecker, darter

Seven species of fruit bat – otherwise known as flying fox – are found on the Indian sub-continent. This rare photograph shows a fruit bat with young feeding on a custard apple.

and many other species. Peacocks strutted everywhere and coveys of quail rose like blown leaves before our jeep. Ranthambhore is best-known for its tigers, but the visitor will see many other mammals too. Besides common langur, spotted deer, Indian gazelle, sambar and nilgai – all of which we saw this particular morning – the park supports leopard, sloth bear, wild boar, porcupine, caracal and a score of other species.

Nature's riches make Ranthambhore a memorable place, but it is the human artefacts which provide the special ingredient that other landscapes often lack. Dominating the park are the ruins of a vast fort, whose four miles of outer walls snake along the purple cliffs which rise dramatically from the valley woodlands. The fort's origins have been traced back to the tenth century and at one time much of central India was ruled from here. The fort's history has been both glorious and gruesome: 10,000 women are said to have committed mass suicide in 1381 rather than be taken by an army of invaders, and in the nineteenth century, when the fort was turned into a prison, inmates were executed by being plied with opium before being hurled over the walls. The forests around the fort are littered with architectural memories, from Hindu temples to decaying mosques, from ruined summer palaces to ancient wells and guard posts. Most have been reclaimed by nature, their walls clothed in creepers and fractured by the searching roots of pipal trees; bats, snakes and lizards have made their homes in the darker recesses of the ruins and tigers lounge in their shade to escape the heat of the midday sun.

In the latter part of the last century, the fort and surrounding forest became the property of the Maharajahs of Jaipur, who built a delightful shooting lodge by the lake and limited hunting to two months in the year. In 1957 Ranthambhore became a wildlife sanctuary and it was elevated to the status of national park in 1974. Today it comes under the umbrella of Project Tiger and over the past two decades the tiger population has almost tripled, from fourteen to forty. Ranthambhore is one of the many protected areas in India which began life as hunting preserves. The area encompassed by Corbett national park was once a favourite hunting ground during colonial times, as was Kanha, one of the finest areas for wildlife in Madhya Pradesh, and Kaziranga in Assam. Sariska national park, a tiger reserve some way north of Ranthambhore, was formerly the hunting preserve of the Maharajahs of Alwar, Bandhargarh fulfilled a similar role for the Maharajahs of Rewa, as did Darrah sanctuary for the princely state of Kota, and Gir – home of the last Asiatic lions – for the Nawabs of Junagadh.

Nearly all of India's significant conservation laws date from the period since independence, although there was some legislative activity during the days of

Much larger than the graceful chital, sambar occur throughout most of India, favouring dense forest in the hill country. This herd relaxes in the lake at Ranthambhore national park.

the Raj. Under various nineteenth-century Forest Acts, the British restricted the hunting rights of forest dwellers (which was grossly unfair) and later divided forests into "shooting blocks"; these were opened and closed in accordance with the abundance or scarcity of game, thus providing a measure of control over the hunting exploits of the wealthy. Occasionally laws were passed to protect a single species whose future was deemed uncertain. The Madras Act of 1873 helped to limit the persecution of Asian elephants in parts of southern India, and the Bengal Rhinoceros Preservation Act of 1932 did the same for the rhino in the north-east. A somewhat more comprehensive piece of legislation was the Wild Birds and Animals Protection Act of 1912, which provided for close seasons, but even this proved inadequate, a fact implicitly recognized by those who argued for the creation of game preserves. By 1928 these covered at least 100,000 square miles of forest land and some areas – for example, Kaziranga – had been given sanctuary status. In 1932 Jim Corbett was made secretary of the newly-formed United Provinces Game Preservation Society, and two years later the United Provinces National Parks Act was passed. In 1936 Hailey national park, later to be renamed after Corbett, became India's first national park, and other areas were given some measure of protection during the short period leading up to the Second World War.

Although independence brought little relief for India's wildlife – huge expanses of forest were engulfed in the "land grab" and the countryside echoed to the sound of guns – the post-war era witnessed great changes in both official and public attitudes towards wildlife. On a global scale, the foundation in 1947 of the International Union for the Conservation of Nature (IUCN) was an event of

*Mrs Indira Gandhi did more than any other politician to help
safeguard India's threatened wildlife.*

considerable significance; at a local level, Nehru's government expressed its good intentions by creating the India Board for Wild Life, which put forward proposals in 1953 for the establishment of eighteen national parks. Individual states passed their own wildlife laws and the first National Parks Act came into force in 1955. Sadly, progress was slow; ten years later India had just nineteen sanctuaries and the total protected area amounted to a mere 2,600 square miles, less than a quarter of a per cent of India's land surface. In the meantime the population was rising rapidly, forests and wild habitats of all types were being exploited as never before, and the list of endangered species became every year more lengthy. During the 1950s the cheetah became extinct in India (although there has been a recent sighting in Andhra Pradesh), and by the 1960s many scientists were voicing fears that before long the tiger would go the same way. It was the fate of the tiger more than any other factor which spurred the Indian government, led by Mrs Indira Gandhi, to introduce new laws to protect the country's remaining wildlife. Mrs Gandhi had helped to launch the Indian branch of the World Wildlife Fund (WWF-I) in 1969, and two years later the WWF began a campaign to save the tiger from extinction. A census carried out in 1972 found that India's tiger population had dropped from an estimated 40,000 early in the century to around 1,800 and the government promptly launched Operation Tiger, which was later to become known as Project Tiger. During the same year, the government passed the Wild Life (Protection) Act.

The rationale behind Project Tiger was simple: the tiger could only be saved if its habitat was protected. "One of the great things about the tiger", explained R. L. Singh, when I met him at the Project Tiger office in New Delhi, "is that it occupies a very wide range of habitats. It shares the same mountain forests as the snow leopard in Himachal Pradesh; it's found in the mangrove swamps of the Sunderbans along with creatures like the saltwater crocodile; and it's equally at home in the arid grasslands of Rajasthan." So Project Tiger is not only protecting the tiger; it is also helping to preserve a great variety of different habitats and a good cross-section of Indian wildlife. Mr Singh had been Director of Project Tiger for six years when I met him, and he admitted that at times the government had been so single-minded in its efforts to conserve the tiger that it had often ignored some unfortunate side-effects: for example, the exclusion of villagers from forests which used to provide them with animal fodder and fuel wood, and the growing incidence of man-eating, which had

India has over 140 species of amphibian. Here a frog displays its genius for camouflage.

become an acute problem around Dudhwa, the Sunderbans and several other parks. "You see," said Mr Singh, "it was a matter of national pride to make Project Tiger succeed. Then we could say to the world, 'Look, not only are we fighting poverty, but our wildlife conservation is second to none too'." There are now eighteen Project Tiger reserves in thirteen states, and between them they cover an area of 10,000 square miles. Measured purely in terms of the welfare of its flagship species, Project Tiger has been a resounding success: the tiger population in India has more than doubled since 1972 to 4,000.

Many other creatures have fared less well. At the latest count, 81 species of mammal, 38 species of bird and 18 species of amphibian and reptile are classified as rare or threatened. Some have become rare because

they have the misfortune to possess something which humans covet. Snow leopard and clouded leopard have been killed for their coats, and although trade in these and many other animal products is now banned both under Indian law and under the Convention on the International Trade in Endangered Species (CITES), poaching continues to threaten their survival in some areas. The smaller cats have suffered too: it takes the skins of thirty fishing cats to make one fur coat, and this secretive marshland hunter is now confined to just a few areas. The fur trade has also led to declines in the numbers of caracal and leopard cat. Prior to the ban on the skin trade in the 1970s, there was a thriving market for reptiles, some of which have never recovered from the exploits of an industry which processed ten million skins a year;

Silent hunters of the undergrowth; India has some 200 species of praying mantis living out a feminist dream: females devour their male partners once the latter have performed their copulatory duties.

the python is one of several species which is still classified as endangered. In southern India male elephants continue to be poached for their ivory (females are tuskless) and this has led to a skewed sex ratio, with females far outnumbering males. Since the turn of the century the great Indian one-horned rhinoceros, which appeared then to be heading for extinction, has increased in numbers, especially in Assam. However, lawlessness and political turmoil in the north-east have been accompanied by a new wave of poaching and over 100 rhinos were killed during the 1980s. Rhino horn is believed to have medicinal, or aphrodisiac, properties; and indeed it is the medicinal use of certain organs which has led to the persecution of several other species like the Indian pangolin, the sloth bear (also valued for its fur and trained to dance by gypsies) and the olive Ridley turtle. In the case of the rare musk deer, it is the perfume industry which is to blame. Although protected by law, poachers continue to hunt musk deer throughout their Himalayan range; a kilogram of musk, which is used as a fixative in the manufacture of perfumes, can fetch as much as $60,000. Poachers are doing well if they get 10 gm of musk from one animal; that does not sound much, but it means that one musk deer is worth more than an average Indian's annual income.

The fate of those animals killed for their skins, tusks, gall bladders or whatever is often well publicized: the trade is gory and brutal and its perpetrators – the poachers and middle men – provide legitimate and readily identifiable targets for those wishing to bring it to an end. However, most of the animals which are classified as rare in India today are suffering not from positive discrimination but from loss of their habitat. This is less newsworthy than stories of poaching, but ultimately of much greater

The Hanuman langur gets its name from the monkey god who helped Rama to defeat one of his enemies. It is the commonest of the five langurs found in the Indian sub-continent and occupies a wide range of habitats, from dense forests to semi-desert. These ones are in Mudamalai wildlife sanctuary.

*Kanha national park in Madhya Pradesh is a stronghold of the
rare southern race of barasingha, or swamp deer.*

consequence. The carving-up of tropical forests has
led to the decline of the hoolock gibbon in Assam,
while the disappearance of jungle pools in the same
area is the main threat to the survival of the white-
winged wood duck. The drainage of wetlands has
worked against swamp and brow-antlered deer, and
the cultivation of grasslands has led to a dramatic
decline in the populations of species as varied as the
great Indian bustard and the Asiatic wild buffalo. The
Nilgiri langur and the lion-tailed macaque are just
two of the mammals whose survival is threatened by
the destruction of their forest habitat in the Western
Ghats, and the loss of upland grasslands has been
largely responsible for the decline in numbers of the
goat-like Nilgiri taur.

Animals and plants cannot survive in isolation
from the habitat in which they have evolved; drain
swamps and the barasingha will disappear; fell the
forests and the lion-tailed macaque will go. In certain
circumstances captive-breeding programmes may
help to swell the populations of an endangered
species, but eventually the animals must be returned
to the wild; it matters not one jot how fecund they
prove to be in the artificial world of the zoo if they no
longer have a home in the outside world. The
protection of large areas of pristine, undisturbed
habitat is therefore a priority in any conservation
strategy and India now has over 70 national parks and
370 wildlife sanctuaries, varying in size from Sanjay
national park in Madhya Pradesh, which spreads
over some 900 square miles of mostly forested land,
to little gems like the watery bird sanctuary of
Keoladeo Ghana, which covers less than twelve
square miles of Rajasthan and can be extensively
explored during the course of a day. The number of
protected areas has risen rapidly – for example, 167
new sanctuaries were created between 1986 and 1990

– and the parks and sanctuaries give protection to at
least one sample of every major habitat type.

However, the park system alone is not enough to
save India's wildlife and prevent scores, or perhaps
hundreds, of species from disappearing over the
coming decades. Less than 5 per cent of India's land
surface has been given protected status, and many
parks and sanctuaries are threatened with despolia-
tion. Even if the management of protected areas were
exemplary, and the authorities successfully prevented
poaching, encroachment, fire-raising, forest clearance and a host of other problems, the protection of
parks and sanctuaries would count for little if all that
lay beyond their boundaries were to disappear. At
present they appear as islands in a sea of trouble.

One of the most respected of India's wildlife
organizations is the Bombay Natural History Society
(BNHS), which was founded in 1883. During its
early years, the BNHS was primarily concerned with
identifying and cataloguing the sub-continent's fauna
and flora. Nowadays it employs a sizeable army of

biologists whose research has an important bearing on conservation policy. The BNHS is especially strong on bird research, and has carried out studies of the great Indian bustard, the lesser florican, the blacknecked crane and many other rare and threatened species. The BNHS has also done important work on the Asian elephant, especially in the south of the country. Being an organization of scientists, the BNHS is not much given to making public pronouncements on environmental issues, and when I met its director, Dr R. B. Grubh, and chief scientist, Mr S. A. Hussain, at the organization's Bombay headquarters, they were eager to stress that the BNHS was not a campaigning group.

We talked for an hour or more about the threats to wild India and my hastily scribbled notes – the director and chief scientist spoke at alarming speed – touch on a great many issues. We began with the coral reefs in the Gulf of Kachchh and around the Nicobar Islands, many of which have been destroyed by mining for construction material and cement, then we moved to Point Calimere, a sanctuary on India's south-east coast. Here, bottom-trawling is having a serious impact on 60,000 hectares of mudflat, a crucial spawning-ground for fish and invertebrates and a major feeding-ground for migratory birds. When it came to discussing the Narmada and other dams, there was a certain wariness; opposition to these colossal structures is seen by those in power as being tantamount to treason and the BNHS does not wish to become embroiled in political controversy. However, Mr Hussain did point out that the Narmada project will cause the destruction of some of Madhya Pradesh's best forests; much of the land to be submerged is covered with forest, and more forest will be cleared to resettle the 100,000 or more people evicted from

their homes to make way for the dams. Dr Grubh then described what he saw as "one of the great tragedies facing the Indian environment" – the loss of the *shola* forests in the Western Ghats. These dense evergreen forests – "they're so dark in places", said Dr Grubh, "that there's scarcely light to read your watch" – were disappearing at an alarming rate. Some of the forest was being cleared to make way for tea, rubber, cardamom and other crops; some was being destroyed by the overgrazing of domestic stock; and some was being lost to shifting cultivation. Things were not much better elsewhere; for example, in Arunachal Pradesh forests were being cleared to provide timber for plywood factories, and in the Andaman Islands they were being felled to accommodate settlers and their families arriving at the rate of 200 a week.

It was hardly surprising that the fate of India's forests took up much of our conversation, for forest – whether dry deciduous, tropical evergreen, montane coniferous or one of a dozen other forest types – is the climax vegetation over much of the country. In other words, were it not for man's activities, both past and present, the Indian subcontinent would be clothed with a dense mantle of green, broken only where high mountains intruded or rivers snaked seawards. Accurate measurements of forest cover are notoriously difficult to gather in developing countries, and indeed many scientists consider the term "deforestation" to be more or less useless, as it describes a multitude of activities from clear-felling to degradation by overgrazing or squatter encroachment. And in any case, when does a forest cease to be a forest – when a quarter of its trees are removed, or half, or all? The following figures give some indication of the rate at which India's forests have been disappearing, but they should be treated

*It is not only rare wildlife that benefits from conservation –
Indian laburnum splashes a painterly yellow across a forest in
the Western Ghats.*

only 11.5 per cent of India is coverd by forest of "adequate density". I met many conservationists who suggested that a figure well below 10 per cent would be nearer the truth.

The fight to save India's remaining forests is discussed in the last chapter, but it is worth stressing the severity of the problem here if only to put the achievements of orthodox conservation policy – and especially the creation of national parks and wildlife sanctuaries – into proper perspective. Obviously, the rate at which forests have disappeared has varied from place to place and from time to time. For example, during the periods 1972–5 to 1980–2 every state in India with the exception of the Andaman and Nicobar Islands and Arunachal Pradesh lost forest; the loss ranged from 0.35 per cent in Nagaland to 15.4 per cent in Sikkim. In 1970 the seven north-easterly states had 55 per cent forest cover; compared to the rest of India, they are still well-covered, but the area under forest had fallen to 42 per cent by 1982 and it has steadily decreased since then. When the British left in 1947 half of Kerala was clothed in dense forest; now less than 15 per cent is forested, and much of this has been heavily degraded by over-grazing and illegal cutting.

The creation of national parks and wildlife sanctuaries is important, but they occupy just a small fraction of the country. The preservation of wild lands, and especially those under forests, is essential both within parks and without. The loss of forests affects not just individual species but India's human population too. Millions of tribal people depend for their survival on the products of the forests in which they live; besides which, the great majority of Indians depend on forests for their supply of fuel wood. To remove the forests from the landscape is rather like destroying the foundations of a building; the destruction

with caution. Estimates suggest that at the turn of the century 40 per cent of India was covered by forest. The latest government figures claim that 23.7 per cent of the Indian land surface is under forest. However, the Ministry of Environment and Forests, which is responsible for the commercial exploitation of forest land as well, paradoxically, as for the conservation of forests and wildlife, concedes that

Spreading the conservation message: a sign beside a highway in Goa (below).

The fragile world of the Upper Indus Valley (right).

IF A SPECIES BECOMES EXTINCT
ITS WORLD WILL NEVER COME
INTO BEING AGAIN IT WILL VANISH
FOREVER LIKE AN EXPLODING STAR
AND FOR THIS WE HOLD DIRECT
RESPONSIBILITY.

DAVID DAY
(1981)

of India's forests, already frighteningly advanced in many areas, could presage a human catastrophe on a scale seldom witnessed before. The writing is already on the wall. In ranges like the Western Ghats the forests act as a sponge. They soak up the rains during the monsoons, then release water gradually throughout the ensuing and lengthy dry period. In the Western Ghats forest destruction has brought about an endless cycle of floods and droughts. During the rainy season the water rushes swiftly off the denuded hills, clogging up dams with eroded top-soil and frequently flooding the valley bottoms. Rivers which once carried water throughout the dry season, thanks to the steady seepage from the forests, have now become seasonal – deliverers of floods during the monsoons; evidence of drought soon after. Over three-quarters of Kerala was declared drought-prone during the years 1983, 1987 and 1988; yet in three other years during the decade – 1981, 1985 and 1989 – the state suffered drastic flooding. Man-made disasters such as these provide the most compelling argument for conservation.

Chapter Four

◆

THE GROWING MULTITUDES

The nearest thing to peace in downtown Bombay comes in the dying hours of the night. By five o'clock in the morning all but the most ardent debauchers have returned to their homes, probably far off in the surrounding sprawl of tenements and slums; and at five o'clock the tens of thousands of homeless who sleep on pavements, in doorways and around the city's stations still have a little time left before the rising sun kick-starts the city back into gaudy motion.

I left my hotel and drank in the strange silence of streets which previously I had known only as polluted, traffic-clogged arteries. Nightwatchmen slept at the foot of gloomy stairwells; bodies lay like flotsam beneath poster-plastered trees; an elderly gentleman hitched up his *dhoti* and emptied his bladder in the gutter outside Churchgate Station. I climbed on board a train to Borivali and as we clattered through the suburbs the carriage swiftly filled with workers, soberly dressed, silent, contemplative for the most part, heading out to the cotton mills in Bombay's outskirts. Dawn came and with it the sights which earlier had been betrayed by their smells: the seams of slum dwellings, children defecating, goats and pigs scrabbling in the filth, and impassive buffaloes, tethered sometimes alone, sometimes in groups, slowly chewing the cud. Occasionally we passed a small plot of paw-paw or banana but never did we escape the cabbagy smells of decay.

People, people everywhere – crowds gather on Bombay's
Chowpatty beach for the Ganesh Chaturthi.

*Scavengers like these vultures in Delhi play a vital role in
cleaning up the mess left by humans.*

Astonishingly, nature had found a niche even here.
There were plenty of scavengers, especially kite and
house crow – a quarter of a million crows are said to
devour eighteen tons of garbage every day in
Bombay – and there were prettier birds too: cattle
egrets, kingfishers, rollers, babblers, and flocks of
waders chasing the receding tide in the fleetingly
glimpsed Mahim Creek.

It took an hour or so to reach Borivali, twenty
miles out from central Bombay, and there I was met
by Sunjoy Monga, a stocky, sallow-faced character
who at the time was deputy editor of *Sanctuary*,
India's leading wildlife magazine. We stopped at a
cafe for a breakfast of *idli*, a southern rice dish, then
headed through the crowded streets to Borivali
national park.

In the dense forest it was hard to see many birds or
mammals but Monga knew them all by their songs
and calls, which he could imitate with remarkable
accuracy. Borivali, he explained, covered little more
than 35 square miles, yet it was home to more
butterflies – over 150 species – than the British Isles,
and some 250 species of bird. Within half an hour we
heard, and in some cases saw, barred jungle owl,
racquet-tailed drongo, emerald dove, several species
of babbler, hoopoe, cormorant and many others.
Langurs and bonnet macaques called eerily from the
trees and our passage was frequently interrupted
as we paused to wipe the dewy webs of wood spiders
from our faces, or side-step the white-shelled crabs
which scuttled silently across the liverwort-slippery
forest floor.

Such was the verdurous tranquillity that we might
have been in the remotest untrodden reaches of the
Western Ghats. Yet some two million people live
within a couple of miles of Borivali's boundary and
perhaps 15 million within twenty miles. A third of

the park, said Monga, fell within the city limits and it was visited by between 1·5 and 2 million people each year, thus making it Asia's most popular national park. A cause for celebration, one would think, especially as so many of Bombay's naturalists began their love affair with nature here. But Monga was pessimistic. "I have grave fears about the future of the park," he said as we walked alongside a picturesque lake which supplied the city with much of its clean drinking water. "Some bureaucrats have already suggested felling the forest to make way for a new township, and every year the problems around the edge get worse."

By ten o'clock we were rattling back towards the city centre in one of Bombay's unroadworthy taxis. Looking back we could see the slums creeping up the forested hills within the national park. From a distance the huts looked like blown litter, yet beneath their crumpled roofs lived men, women and children with aspirations and requirements like the rest of us. And what they needed was space and food and a place to live and fuel with which to cook. Small wonder, then, that many cross into the national park to chop firewood; small wonder if every year the shanties creep further into the forest. For middle-class visitors from Bombay, and for foreigners like myself, Borivali gives wonderful relief from the noise and dirt of the city, but to those who scratch a living around its periphery it is much more than a playground, and it possesses its own peculiar dangers. Between 1987 and 1991, leopards caught and killed six children. Inevitably, the locals had avenged these deaths whenever the opportunity arose. Monga described how a large gang had recently surrounded a leopard and beaten it to death with sticks and stones. To these people, survival of the family is more important than wildlife conservation.

Borivali national park, on the outskirts of Bombay, boasts as good an example of tropical forest as can be found anywhere along the west coast. However, its future is uncertain (below).

Cups-and-saucers: this aptly named plant can be seen in the forest around Bombay (right).

*(Overleaf.) India is a nation of crowds: every year vast numbers
of pilgrims flock to the holy River Ganges at Varanasi.*

Borivali has yet to be overwhelmed by people; but before long it may be, just as so many other patches of woodland and marsh and mudflat around Bombay have been invaded and covered with concrete and shanties. At the turn of the century the population of Bombay stood at under a million. By the beginning of the Second World War, it had doubled to 1·8 million; by 1966 it was 5·4 million; by 1981, 8·2 million; and the census of 1991 put the population at over 11 million. The latest projections suggest that Bombay may have 17 million inhabitants by the end of this century, though it is hard to see where the extra 5 or 6 million will go; over half the population already lives in slums and a further 2 million occupy dwellings which have neither tapped water nor private latrines. No one seems to know how many homeless there are: a survey in 1972 suggested 62,000, of which the vast majority were young males who had come in search of work; there could be three times that many today.

Bombay's growth has been even more spectacular than India's as a whole, as it is a sum of both natural increase and immigration from other parts of the country. I had met many people before I arrived in Bombay who suggested that virtually all the environmental and social ills which plagued the country were a direct consequence of population growth; after all, there are more than three times as many Indians alive today as there were at the turn of the century. However, I had met others – admittedly a minority – who said that this was an irrelevance; that twice the present population of 850 million could be fed and housed were resources and opportunities shared more equitably. Most people concerned with development issues felt that the country urgently needed to reduce population growth – Indians now constitute one-sixth of the world's population, yet they are confined to little more than 2 per cent of its land mass – and, at the same time, create a fairer society. Indeed, the former, one could argue, follows naturally from the latter.

The Family Planning Association of India (FPAI) was set up in 1949 in Bombay, and it now has some 1,650 paid staff, over 3,000 volunteers and 41 branches. I met Dr Seshagiri Rao, its assistant secretary-general and a small, portly man of great charm and lively intelligence, in his offices in Nariman Point. The first thing he said was, "Population growth and environmental problems are intricately related – that's our main theme now." Before we set off for the infamous Dharavi slums we talked around the issue of population for a couple of hours. This is not a subject where one progresses with inexorable certitude, like a skilled barrister, from carefully marshalled evidence to logical conclusion, for it touches on so many aspects of human life – literacy, child health, education, the status of women. . . .

When the FPAI was set up, life expectancy in India was twenty-seven years, and the average woman gave birth to at least eight children during her lifetime; today life expectancy is nudging sixty and on average Indian women have four children. So great progress has been made, though at the present rate of growth, India's population will double in just thirty-seven years. "Communication is a major problem," said Dr Rao. "There are fourteen accepted national languages and the number of dialects runs into hundreds." And, of course, illiteracy makes it harder to get the family planning message across to many people. "It was rampant when India became independent," said Dr Rao. "I'm not blaming the British, but when they left only 14 per cent of the population was literate. There's been a big improvement since then, especially among men." Around 64 per cent of India's men are now thought to be literate, and perhaps 40 per cent of women.

In 1990 Dr Rao was awarded the prestigious Better World Medal (as were Lech Walesa and Greenpeace International) and the citation highlighted his work "involving the village people of India in strengthening family planning, improving the status of women, and reducing poverty and illiteracy". He told me about a project he helped to set up in some seventy villages to the east of Bombay: "You see, women contribute so much to the economy, but their position in society is very low – so women's status is a crucial concern. In one of the villages the women have got together to influence all aspects of village life. And do you know, they've been so successful that even the men are impressed and the elected *panchayat* – the council – is now dominated by women. The women have even set up banking facilities to stop exploitation by money-lenders." Such a situation is almost unheard-of in the rest of the country.

In some parts of India population growth has slowed dramatically. "The south is doing much better than the north," explained Dr Rao. The state of Kerala provides the classic family planning success story: during the decade 1981–91 the population grew by just 14 per cent; this compared with 23 per cent for Bihar, 28 per cent for Rajasthan and 25 per cent for Uttar Pradesh. Several factors hindered the family planning effort in these backward northern states. "Illiteracy is a major problem working against family planning," said Dr Rao, "and besides that and poor education generally, the state governments are not giving enough support to birth control or health programmes, and there is a huge gap between the rich and the poor. . . . There's terrible human degradation in many parts of the north." In Kerala 90 per cent of the population is literate, whereas in Bihar, Rajasthan and Uttar Pradesh literacy hovers around a meagre 40 per cent, with women at the bottom of the educational heap. In rural Bihar, 90 per cent of adult women cannot read or write, and among the poorest fifth of the rural population, illiteracy is almost univeral. "Educationally", suggested the *Economist* in a recent survey of the country, "much of India's vast rural hinterland has been left to rot."

This was the clear message when we visited the Dharavi slums, an hour's drive from the city centre and one of the first sights to greet international travellers landing at Santa Cruz airport. Dharavi, says one popular guidebook, is "one hell of an introduction to urban India at its worst". Well, yes and no. There are probably 500,000 people living in these slums, some in conditions of unspeakable poverty, though no worse than those experienced by countless millions of the very poor in Delhi or Calcutta or, for that matter, in parts of the Indian countryside. Crammed into shacks often constructed

*Defusing the population bomb: better to breed prudently than
profusely, suggests a family planning poster.*

from little more than discarded wood and canvas,
people sleep, eat and conduct all the affairs of family
life within a pace or two of polluting industries and
open sewers.

But life is by no means univerally grim. Dr Rao
and I were accompanied by Mrs Padma Srinivasan,
the FPAI's assistant field director, and a younger
woman who worked as a health worker in Dharavi.
"I love my job," announced the latter, unprompted.
"I love working in the slums." We clattered along the
rutted streets into the heart of Dharavi and pulled up
outside the Subhas Chandra Bose Cooperative
Housing Society. Coops, explained Mrs Srinivasan,
had a better chance of getting land than private
individuals and there were many in Bombay like this
one, housing perhaps 500 to 1,000 people. To the
passing traveller, the shabby housing all looks much
the same, but the drabness masks a great diversity of
peoples and cultures. This particular colony consisted
entirely of immigrants from Karnataka, and they all
spoke their native language, Kannada; further along
the road there was a Tamil-speaking colony; and
beyond that a Punjabi colony. We were shown into a

small hall where three beautiful girls with scented
jasmine in their blue-black hair were learning to sew
on treadle machines. Two men in their twenties
came to talk to us. Apparently, the late Rajiv Gandhi
had visited Dharavi a few years ago and ordered a
special house-building programme for slum-dwellers.
The young men said they would be happy if their
hutments were knocked down and they were moved
to better accommodation, but they wanted to stay
together; nobody would tolerate the community
being split up. I asked one of the men whether he was
happy here; had Bombay turned out as well as he had
hoped when he left the countryside? "Oh yes, we're
much better off here," he replied vigorously. "We
have jobs, there are good schools for our children and
we've got proper health care. . . . In the countryside
we had no work . . . just farming and sleep, farming
and sleep. It was terribly dull . . . here we are
comfortable."

We looked into one of the hutments. It consisted of
a single room 12 foot square. A naked child slept on
the concrete floor. A bed made of wooden boards
occupied most of one wall; the bedding was neatly
folded away in an alcove. There was a small sink
opposite the door, and on the shelf above there were
rows of gleaming aluminium pots and two beautifully polished brass primus stoves. An old-fashioned
battery clock ticked away above a little Christian
shrine with a crucifix, a picture of Jesus and some
fresh flowers. This room was home to a family of
six, and it was typical of the colony.

From here we wandered down streets so narrow
that two people could scarcely pass without breath-
ing in. In some shacks groups of men were making
leather goods; in one, three girls were attaching tiny
sparkling discs to polyester saris; in a large hall forty
or so children – all beautifully turned out – were

*Every day several hundred people leave their rural homes and
descend on the slums of Bombay. City life has many attractions:
a wage economy, good schools, reasonable health care, the
excitement of the cinema . . . (below).*

Doing the best they can – slum-dwellers in Bombay (right).

chanting poetry with their teacher. Many outsiders
speak of Dharavi as if it were the abode of the
damned, a place of eternal hopelessness. Parts are
dreadful, but this colony was full of vitality, laughter
and optimism.

Every day some 300 to 400 new arrivals swell the
numbers in the city slums. Most come in search of
work, and most have left the countryside. The new
arrivals further strain the city's capacity to supply its
inhabitants with shelter, water and electricity; but,
just as significantly, the expanding cities place ever–
increasing strains on India's rural resources. Forty

miles north of Bombay is Dahuna *taluka*, an oasis of
productive land sandwiched between the giant
industrial complexes of northern Maharashtra and
southern Gujarat. Dahuna provides over a quarter of
Bombay's fruit and flowers and is sometimes referred
to as its garden. It has 130,000 hectares of forest,
5,000 hectares of orchard, and the area provides a
livelihood for tens of thousands of farmers and
fishermen. But this is no paradise. The forests are
rapidly being depleted as teak is felled to supply
building timber for neighbouring towns, and every
year large areas are razed to satisfy the growing

demands for fuel. It is said that as a result of deforestation the annual rainfall has declined from 150 inches in the 1960s to 75 inches today, and ground water resources are two thirds of what they used to be. Soil fertility has steadily declined and the yield of one of the major crops, chickoo, has fallen by 40 per cent over the last decade. The demand for natural resources is placing an unsustainable burden on Dahuna, which is being further despoiled by industrial development. Eighty per cent of India's rubber balloons are manufactured in 40 to 50 units here, employing child labour on a large scale and polluting both air and water.

At present, every one million acres of land in India supports around one million people; by the end of the century the same area will have to support 1·2 million and in thirty to forty years perhaps double that number. Over the next ten years the demand for foodgrains will rise from 146 million tonnes a year to 238 million tonnes; for pulses from 12 million tonnes to 33 million. At present the country consumes 100 million tonnes of firewood each year; it will need three or four times that much by the year 2000. Industry, too, will demand more from the country-side: half of India's industrial output uses raw materials – fibre crops like cotton and jute; timber for the paper and plywood industries; limestone and gravel for the building industry; rubber, palm oil and numerous other crops – and all these require or consume land. Nature, already in retreat, will inevitably suffer as farmers and foresters, miners and fishermen, industrialists and poachers go about their daily business. People will continue to drift from the countryside into the cities. The urban population is expected to rise from 155 million today to 350 million by the year 2000 – and at the same time the consumer aspirations of the rural multitudes will become increasingly sophisticated (60 per cent of all motorcycles now go to the rural market, although urban luxuries are far beyond the means of most, 1989's five best-sellers being toilet soap, washing soap cakes, detergents, batteries and packaged tea).

In the backward villages, where education and health care are rudimentary or non-existent, men (in particular) and women favour large families. Children provide free labour at home and on the land, and the parents look to their offspring to provide them with food, shelter and care in their old age. Children, in other words, provide a degree of security. Wherever infant mortality is high, as it is in rural India, people are unlikely to think in terms of smaller families, even if help and advice is readily available. So the population will continue to rise, and every year India's wildlands will be further diminished.

From the Cardamom Hills in the deep south to the Himalaya in the north, the uplands bear the scars of overpopulation. Every year the poor, the landless and the plain greedy extend the limits of cultivation, carving fields and terraces from land which previous generations had left as forest, knowing its soils to be too fragile, its slopes too steep. The Nilgiris have probably suffered as much as any of the hill regions. "In fifty years' time there will be nothing left," said Mr Radcliffe despairingly. "I simply can't see how you're going to stop everything disappearing." Ruddy-skinned, silver-haired and very British in his manner, Mr Radcliffe spent an hour, one brisk, sunny morning in Ootacamund, telling me why he felt his beloved Nilgiri Hills were doomed. At the heart of the matter lies India's burgeoning population. "By the end of the century," he explained, "there'll be 1,000 million people in India and by 2030 we'll have a population of 1,500 million. People are like a river – a river finds its way wherever it's convenient to go . . . and people will always choose the Nilgiris ahead of the arid plains as a place to settle."

For many years, explained Mr Radcliffe, settlers from the lowlands and from cities like Madras and Mysore had been chipping terraces out of the steep hillsides near his home, which was stunningly situated on the edge of the plateau, overlooking the national park of Mudamalai and the plains beyond. He spoke of the settlers with great respect: "They're so resourceful and industrious. They come with nothing, and in a short while they have cleared the trees, planted some crops and established themselves." But sadly, this squatter encroachment of the Nilgiris is leading to their destruction.

Most of the land in rural India falls under the heading of "revenue land", and is thus ear-marked for exploitation; a smaller area is defined as *patta*, or privately owned land; and finally there is the land classified as "forest". The latter category is strictly protected (in theory, if not in practice) but this will not save all of India's forests, for the simple reason that much of the forest is classified as "revenue", rather than "forest" land. "The problem here", explained Mr Radcliffe, "is that anyone can squat on revenue land, and they won't be turned out. In any case, if they were evicted, they'd just settle elsewhere. So they end up being fined a nominal sum, and then after a while the district collector will give them the land they've squatted as *patta*." A few years ago the collector in Ooty had the power to issue around 1,000 permits for *patta* during his three-year tenure of office. One of Ooty's past collectors is said to have given ten times as many, nearly all on forested land and many to Tamil refugees from Sri Lanka. At one point Badaga tribals threatened to take up arms against the newcomers, so furious were they about the damage caused to the hills. According to

Mr Radcliffe, most of the hills around Ooty have now been encroached; quite simply, there are too many people.

Wherever you go in the Nilgiris you will see plumes of smoke rising from the hills, the tell-tale sign of forests being cleared and burned, either to be squatted or transformed into tea plantations or commercial forests. The worst destruction in recent times has taken place in the long valleys around Attapadi, in the western Nilgiris, but the problem affects every district and makes a mockery of the hand-painted posters, sponsored by the Forest Department and dotted around the towns, which portentously declare, "Forest and trees – a solid solution to Global Warming". The consequences of all this destruction are becoming all too apparent. Animals and birds are the first to suffer, and as their habitats diminish, so do their numbers. One hundred and fifty years ago, tiger, jungle sheep, gaur or Indian bison, bear, leopard and elephant were all common in the forests round Ooty. The elephant has been driven off the higher hills, as has the tiger; most of the other creatures have either retreated to the small patches of native forest which have yet to be cleared, or they have disappeared altogether. Deforestation on the steeper slopes has been accompanied, inevitably, by an increase in the frequency of landslides. During one monsoon recently, over forty people were killed when a river of mud, no longer restrained by the mesh of tree roots, swept dwellings and crops down a hillside. So severe is the problem of erosion that dozens of lorries are now permanently employed taking silt – the former top-soil of the Nilgiris – out of the Bhavani Sagar, a dam into which many of the region's stream and rivers flow.

Mr Radcliffe is one of the main contributors to a vigorous little newsletter called *Tahr*, published by the Nilgiri Wildlife and Environment Association. The editorial of the issue which had just appeared at the time of my visit began as follows:

The ever-increasing growth of the population in Asia, resulting in a vast number of persons spreading out over lands previously unoccupied must inevitably result in pollution – this is inescapable and must be understood and accepted in any discussion or in the planning of the regulation of human activities. It is a Fact."

The author – Mr Radcliffe, I imagine – goes on to say that while Nature usually takes care of any imbalance, the human race does not, and there follows a list of avoidable pollution in Ooty, which includes:

"– The waste products of the human body . . .
– The disgustingness of waste paper and office rubbish thrown out from the telecommunications buildings at Ooty.
– The muck outside every roadside coffee shop.
– The bullock-cart stand at the Ooty market."

Sorting out pollution such as this requires no money, "just an understanding of what pollution means". This is brave stuff, because many Indians are exceedingly touchy about the subject of pollution, especially when it embraces personal hygiene. James Cameron, in his delightful book *An Indian Summer*, observed that:

"V. S. Naipaul deeply outraged the Indian Establishment by the strictures and comments in his book *An Area of Darkness*, but probably most of all by his obsessive distaste with the Indians' carefree attitude to the emptying of their entrails. 'Indians defecate everywhere. They defecate, mostly, by railway tracks. But they also defecate on the beaches; they defecate on the hills; they defecate by the river banks; they defecate on the streets; they never look for cover . . ." V. S. Naipaul gave much consideration to this phenomenon, as indeed it is difficult not to do to something the evidence of which is so pervasive."

The casual evacuation of bowels may be of no great import where humans are scattered lightly across the landscape, but in a nation where people congregate in great densities it poses a severe health hazard. Gastroenteritis, parasitic infestation, typhoid and dozens of other diseases – many life-threatening, especially to babies and young children – are caused by drinking water polluted by human faeces. Wandering along a railway track or beside a river is a perilous occupation, and although India has 3,500 miles of coast it is astonishing how many beaches are daily defiled. One of the most shocking places I visited was the fishing village of Vizhinjam, on Kerala's southern tip. Here thousands of poor fisherfolk (this is an Indian archaism, not mine) and their families are crammed into slums as appalling as almost any to be seen in the big cities. The bay in front of the slums is strewn with canoes – and human turds. You need the pirouetting skills of a ballet dancer to make it down to the water without mishap. Apparently, the entire female population of Vizhinjam gets up at four o'clock in the morning to do their business, and they are followed shortly after by the men. There are, it must be said, certain aspects of Indian lavatorial behaviour which are thoroughly praiseworthy: were

*A familiar sight in India: belching factories conjure up a
Lowryesque hell.*

850 million people to adopt the western habit of using toilet paper, rather than water, the environmental consequences, in terms of the forests which would have to be felled to meet the new demand, would be quite appalling.

The most curious aspect of all this is that Indians must be the cleanest people in the world. Even the poorest person, in the grimiest slum, pays scrupulous attention to the daily rituals of cleansing the body and you seldom see an Indian in filthy clothes. Anyway, the point must be made that the human waste of getting on for 850 million people – and even in Delhi, there are six million living in dwellings without

sewers – is a cause of much pollution, damaging to the health of both humans and wildlife. This is, as *Tahr* would say, a 'Fact'; and as the population rises it will get worse unless something is done.

And something is being done to clean up the pollution which disfigures and corrupts the loveliest and holiest of rivers, Mother Ganga. There are over 100 towns dotted along the banks of the 1,580-mile long river; over a quarter of these have populations in excess of 100,000, and all have undergone dramatic growth over the past half-century or so. For example, the population of Bihar's capital, Patna, rose from 475,000 in 1971 to 814,000 in 1986. Varanasi,

A child contemplates the discarded flowers and festival rubbish
in the River Hooghly, Calcutta.

Allahabad, Kanpur and many other towns have swelled too, and all these settlements deliver into the river huge quantities of raw sewage. The river also acts as a sink for untreated industrial effluent, for pesticide run-off, and for animal carcasses and half-burnt human corpses. Such pollution is by no means a recent phenomenon. In 1864 the president of Bengal's Sanitary Commission wrote that every year 5,000 bodies, many thrown into the River Hooghly by hospitals, could be found in water used by the people of Calcutta for washing and drinking. However, pollution levels have steadily risen parallel to the growth in population.

It is hard to say how the pollution has affected the river's wildlife. Many of the mammals and reptiles of the river Ganges are threatened by factors other than pollution, although pollution may not be helping their cause. For example, dam-building and river canalization have led to a decline in the numbers of Gangetic dolphins, while the long-snouted crocodile, the gharial, has been persecuted almost to the point of extinction by hunters after its skin. Eleven species of turtle inhabit the Ganges, and many of these have become endangered as they provide a cheap source of protein to villagers living beside the river. Back in 1822, Francis Hamilton-Buchanan published *An Account of fishes found in the River Ganges and its branches* – 269 of them altogether. Many of these fishes, together with a great wealth of insects, shellfish, crabs, worms and other lowly creatures are adversely affected by pollution, and much to the government's credit it has decided to take action.

The Ganga Action Plan was launched in 1986. One of its main objectives was to intercept and treat 875 million litres of sewage per day – out of the 1,400 generated – in twenty-five major cities and towns. By 1991 schemes initiated by the plan were treating almost 400 million litres a day, so progress had been made. Getting on for 3,000 public lavatories and 41,000 individual flush latrines had also been built under a Low Cost Sanitation Programme, and by 1991, nineteen electric crematoria had begun operation, while many riverside ghats had been renovated and cleaned. The authorities had also set up turtle hatcheries in Lucknow and Varanasi, and 2,500 of these scavenging reptiles, with their strong taste for the dead flesh of humans and animals, had been released into Mother Ganga.

Five hundred miles downstream of Varanasi, shortly before its confluence with the Brahmaputra, the Ganges fragments into a dozen separate strands, each meandering its own idiosyncratic way through the fertile delta towards the Bay of Bengal. Like some primaeval sea-creature, the Ganges has many mouths, one of the largest of which belongs to the Hooghly, on whose banks sprawls Kipling's "City of Dreadful Night". Calcutta, he wrote, was a city "where the cholera, the cyclone, and the crow come and go, by the sewerage rendered foetid, by the sewer made impure". Few places have received such a bad press, but if you search beyond the wretchedness you will find that Calcutta has many virtues. There is a warmth among the people which one more commonly associates with a village than a city, and the native Bengalis possess a wit and intelligence which make commerce-obsessed Bombay and parochial Delhi seem shallow and dull. It is true that the public services in Calcutta – whether of transport, telecommunications, power supply or sewerage – are by any standards an absolute disgrace, but the situation is not unremitting bleak, for the city possesses a system for disposing of some of its waste products which is among the most enlightened in the world. This, I should add swiftly, is no thanks to

The East Calcutta Marshes – sewage works, fish farms and vegetable gardens all in one. The marshes are now threatened by developers.

West Bengal's communist government nor to any high-tech wizardry introduced by sanitary engineers.

On the day of my arrival the magazine *India Today* ran a short piece entitled "Sewage Nightmare – Calcutta in eco-peril". The article suggested that if the East Calcutta Marshes were developed for building, as some wished, the city would smother in its own sewage. A few days later, I went to see Dr Dhrubajyoti Ghosh, a sanitary engineer who had incurred the wrath of the state government by mounting a vigorous campaign to save the marshes. The East Calcutta Marshes, he explained, constituted the largest and finest traditional sewage and waste-disposal system in the world. Dr Ghosh estimated that a third of the city's sewage ended up in the marshes to be processed in the most ingenious ways. Thirty square miles of marshland, or just under 7,500 acres, is taken up by sewage-fed fish ponds or *bheris*. Each year these fisheries produce 7,500 tons of fish and they are among the most productive in India. While some of the sewage goes straight to the *bheris*, some is detained for use on the "garbage farms". Much of Calcutta's refuse is dumped on the fringe of the marshes and picked over by several thousand people; some collect plastic bottles, some tin cans, others canvas or string or metal. By the time they have finished, all that is left is organic matter which, when irrigated with treated sewage, forms a fertile substratum for vegetable farming. Every day Calcutta gets around 150 tons of vegetables from these marshes. The effluent from the fish ponds is also put to good use, mainly in the rice paddies. "It is a system of genius," explained Dr Ghosh, "and it's perfectly suited to countries in the developing world: the two basic requirements seem to be poverty and sunshine, and we have plenty of both." Several governments in south-east Asia had asked Dr Ghosh

to plan similar wetland waste-disposal systems beside their big cities, and his design for a sewage disposal unit, based on the Calcuttan model, had recently been introduced to three municipalities along the Ganges. "I take great pride in this naive, simple system," he said.

Over the years the wetlands have diminished in size as the city has expanded eastward. Much was lost to the Salt Lake housing project in the 1960s, and the more recent construction of the Eastern Metropolitan Bypass has brought the wetlands within closer reach

of developers, both public and private. Calcutta is a notoriously corrupt city, and those battling to save the marshes have been subject to all manner of intimidation. If the building lobby gets its way, Calcutta may gain some fancy housing and a new exhibition ground, but it will lose one of the most efficient and productive waste management schemes imaginable. On present evidence the municipality is scarcely able to look after the most rudimentary services; it certainly could not afford the sort of mechanical sewage system which would be required

were this natural one to be destroyed. Calcuttans, incidentally, would also lose a wonderful area of green, unpolluted land, the workplace of 20,000 people and home to scores of species of waterbirds and to mammals like jackal, marsh mongoose and palm civet. In India's expanding cities, the links between man and nature become yearly more tenuous: the East Calcutta Marshes provide a glorious exception, with the fish- and vegetable-farmers – or "natural ecologists" as Dr Ghosh calls them – doing the people of the city an immense favour.

Chapter Five

ISLANDS IN A SEA OF TROUBLE

It took us a little over an hour to descend several thousand feet from the breezy heights of the Nilgiris to the Moyar River and the undulating plains of Mudamalai. The vegetation which ran beside the river was thick and verdurous, but most of the forest was parched, the trunks and branches of teak and silk-cotton lichen-grey above the ochres and tarnished coppers of the stringy grassland. In a month's time the monsoon rains would transform this wildlife sanctuary, clothing the trees once again with a thick canopy of green and stimulating the grasslands into lush life. And once again, the elephants would be on the move. Mudamalai lies within the state of Tamil Nadu and occupies a lozenge of land immediately to the north of the Nilgiris. It forms part of a much larger complex which includes Nagarahole and Bandipur national parks in Karnataka and Wynad wildlife sanctuary in Kerala. Together they take up a good chunk of the Nilgiri Biosphere Reserve and they boast a magnificent mix of forests, grasslands, river gorges and hill country. This diversity of habitat is reflected in the region's rich flora and fauna. Tigers and leopards prey on sambar, muntjac, chital and mouse deer, and the area supports important populations of those two great herbivores, the Asian elephant and the gaur, or Indian bison.

At least 40,000 Asian elephants were killed or captured during the past century. Loss and fragmentation of their forest habitat poses the greatest threat to their survival today.

A highly mobile population of some 1,500 elephants ranges through these forests. During the dry season the animals cluster around a small number of water-rich areas, but once the monsoon arrives they disperse evenly throughout the region. "This is when the problems happen," explained Mohanraj of the Nilgiri Wildlife and Environment Association. "After the rains the elephants will raid the croplands. Every year people are killed trying to chase them off, and inevitably elephants are killed too." One of the more gruesome methods used to dispatch the animals involves planting dynamite in jackfruit, a great delicacy for elephants. Man–elephant conflicts, as they are prosaically known, are on the increase, and they are destined to become more frequent and more violent in the future.

Not long ago the elephants had a broad corridor of land through which to move on their migrations, stretching from the Moyar Gorge in the north to the slopes of the Nilgiris in the south. Gradually the width of the migration corridor has been reduced. Forests have been cleared to make way for crops and in some places elephant-proof fences have been erected. Perhaps the greatest cause of man–elephant conflict today comes from the growth of Masinagudi, a town on the southern edge of the sanctuary. A decade or so ago this was a small village with a few cattle herders; now it is a boom-town and its unplanned growth threatens the future of not just the elephant, but the whole of Mudamalai.

At the time of my visit, the Electricity Board was planning to create a new township to house the work-force employed on the building of the Pykara Ultimate State Hydro-electric Project. If built as planned, the township will attract another 2,000 permanent settlers as well as 1,000 temporary labourers. Masinagudi's present population of 5,000 could thus easily double.

Each day the workers will be bussed to the construction site at Singara, some five miles away, directly across the thin strip of land through which the elephants must now migrate. "One can only guess at the problems we'll get then," said Mohanraj as we inspected a grim labour camp on the outskirts of town. He conceded that the hydro-electric scheme would bring some benefits to Tamil Nadu, "but these are far outweighed by the costs". The Nilgiri Wildlife and Environment Association is one of many organizations opposed to the Electricity Board's plans. The World Wide Fund for Nature (India), the Bombay Natural History Society and the Forestry Department have also expressed displeasure, but so far to little avail. However, these groups have undoubtedly had a restraining influence on some developments in and around the sanctuary. It was following their vigorous campaigning that plans to build a huge tourist complex were dropped; they also managed to force the closure of a newly built electro-plating factory outside Masinagudi, which would not only have sucked up must of the Moyar River's flow, but discharged back into it considerable quantities of cyanide.

"It's only a question of time before Mudamalai goes," suggested one of the conservationists I met there. This is conjecture, of course, although there is plenty of evidence to support so bleak a view. The Government of India has made tremendous strides in the field of wildlife conservation: the number of protected areas has steadily risen and by the end of 1991 there were over 70 national parks and 370 wildlife sanctuaries; in official circles there is even talk of increasing the network of parks and sanctuaries to 148 and 503 respectively. However, the very survival of many protected areas is threatened by overgrazing, illegal felling, poaching, fire-raising, terrorism and industrial development. India's protected areas have become islands in a sea of trouble, and the tensions which exist between those who manage them and those who live beside them become daily more acute. It is not just the wildlife which suffers, but the human population too: insensitive conservation policies frequently deprive villagers of their livelihoods, and in certain areas carnivores deprive them of their lives. Unless the tensions which presently exist are swiftly defused, we may well see the day when government finds itself in the business of descheduling parks and sanctuaries – admitting, in effect, the impracticality of its policies. No two parks or sanctuaries suffer – or, for that matter, thrive – in precisely the same way; and no two communities living in or around protected areas are confronted by an identical set of problems. The only general rule, as George Bernard Shaw once remarked, is that there are no general rules. All the same, one can identify certain key activities which threaten the future of many parks and sanctuaries.

INDIA'S BELEAGUERED PARKS

Broadly speaking, there are three ways in which forests are being degraded or destroyed in India: by fire, by felling (illegal or otherwise) and by overgrazing, which is the most significant threat in many areas. Consider Mudamalai and the surrounding countryside: twenty years ago there were about 5,000 cattle in the around Masinagudi; today there are over 20,000 and they are eating the forests out of existence. A little way to the south of Masinagudi, Mohanraj and I drove off the main road and followed a dirt track which took us to the foot of the Nilgiris.

Not long ago this had been a dry deciduous forest; now it was almost totally denuded of trees. The monsoon rains of previous years had opened up wide gullies, in places twenty feet across and over ten feet deep. This would not have happened had it not been for the clearance of forest and subsequent overgrazing by cattle. The cattle provide no meat and scarcely any milk, their only function being to transform plant matter into dung, which is sold to farmers in Kerala. The beneficiaries of this strange industry – the transferring of fertility from one region to another – are few; most of the cattle are owned by businessmen who live in distant cities, and the herders and dung-collectors make no more than a subsistence living.

By the time we drove into Mudamalai wildlife sanctuary it was early evening. Langurs and macaques scampered beside the road and the birdlife celebrated the cooling of the day with fluty songs and raucous calls: peacocks and jungle fowl strutted among thick stands of bamboo, while mynahs, parakeets, drongos and babblers sang and chattered among the higher foliage. While the sanctuary's wildlife prepared for the coming of night, herd after herd of long-horned, hump-backed cattle trudged their way back towards Masinagudi. Many consisted of little more than tough hides slung across a rack of ribs, and it was clear that at this time of year even the wildlife sanctuary failed to supply them with ample fodder. It came as a shock to realize that these slow, placid creatures, and the progeny of this and future generations, will, unless restrained, destroy the forests of Mudamalai and many other protected areas.

The increase in India's cattle herd is to some extent a function of the rising human population, which in itself threatens the integrity of many protected areas. The population factor is especially significant in the

These placid-looking creatures threaten to destroy Mudamalai
wildlife sanctuary (below left).

Goats cause tremendous damage to upland forests. A large herd
in Himachal Pradesh (lower left).

Gangetic plain, the fertile region which occupies a tenth of India's land surface and supports a third of its inhabitants. At one time the Gangetic plain was clothed in forest, interspersed among which were patches of marsh and grassland. Nine tenths of the plain has been converted into cropland and the survival of the remaining patches of natural habitat is by no means assured. In fact, less than 1·4 per cent of the Gangetic plain – compared to a national average

*Modern India is hungry for land: each year forests are felled to
make way for crops, marshes are drained to grow more food.
Even in the remote mountain regions of Himachal Pradesh,
agricultural cultivation eats into the wilderness (below).*

of 5 per cent – is protected, with most of the parks
and sanctuaries being concentrated in the *terai*, the
thin belt of forest and grassland which stretches along
the foothills of the Himalaya. Three of India's best
known national parks, Dudhwa, Corbett and Rajaji,
are found here, and a tide of humanity threatens to
engulf them.

Rajaji national park is a short distance from Dehra
Dun, home of the admirable Wildlife Institute of
India, a government body founded in 1982. The
institute is run by H. S. Panwar, a former director of
Project Tiger, and it is staffed by a team of talented
ecologists led by Dr A. J. T. Johnsingh. Dr Johnsingh
is a tall, imposing-looking Tamil who began his
career studying wild dogs, or dholes, in Bandipur in
the 1970s. He then worked on babblers and the
Indian fox and spent some time at the Smithsonian
Institute in the United States before joining the
Bombay Natural History Society, for whom he
conducted studies on the Asian elephant in
Mudamalai. He came to the institute in 1985 and has
since spent much of his time studying the wildlife
and people of Rajaji national park. "You can't ignore
the population issue," was one of the first things he
said when I met him at the institute.

Between 1951 and 1981 the population around
Rajaji more than doubled, from 189,000 to 410,000,
and during this period 27 square miles of forest was
razed to make way for new townships and development projects. "Habitat loss has been one problem,"
explained Dr Johnsingh, "but habitat degradation is
just as significant." He cited the spread of unpalatable
plants as an example. Approximately 5,000 gujjars,
nomadic graziers who came here from Jammu
several centuries ago, live within the boundaries of
the national park with between 5,000 and 10,000
buffaloes; these animals depend on the park for their

*Many of India's tribal peoples have suffered as their forest
homelands have been invaded by settlers, commercial foresters,
dam-builders and others. Gond tribals on the move.*

Tribal people still practice jhum *(slash-and-burn) agriculture in many of India's forests. In some places the* jhum *cycle has been reduced from fifty years to five or six. The forest and soil inevitably suffer.*

fodder requirements, as do a similar number of livestock from the villages around the periphery. Their grazing habits have caused a decline in the density of edible plants and a corresponding rise in that of unpalatable species. The gujjars have also made their presence felt in other ways: they cut large quantities of wood, which they use both for cooking and for heating, and they lop trees to supply fodder for their livestock. This practice has already had an effect on the populations of fruit-eating mammals and birds.

The issue of what to do about tribal practices has been vexing conservationists for a long time. Other- wise known as *adivasis* – or the "original people" – India's sixty-five million tribals have traditionally made their living from the forests. They have had a rough time of it over the past few centuries and "civilization", as we are pleased to call it, has seldom treated them kindly. Very few tribals remain un- disturbed in their forest habitat; most have been dispossessed of their land, and by the government's own admission nearly ten million have been dis- placed by development projects – dams, roads, hydro-power schemes – in the last forty years. All too often, the former forest dwellers have drifted into the city slums, and many of those who have remained in the countryside have failed to adapt to their changed circumstances. Shortly before I visisted the *terai*, I spent time in the Narmada Valley, where 100,000 or more people, most of them tribals, are set to be displaced by the building of a series of dams. "These people are dependent on jungle, just as fish are on water," said one anti-dam campaigner, who went on to talk in glowing terms about tribal life. "The *adivasis* live in harmony with nature," he suggested. "They understand the forests and they know how to use them without destroying them." I

repeated this conversation to Dr Johnsingh. "Fifty years ago, the tribals might have co-existed peace- fully with nature," he replied, "but to talk of tribals living in harmony with the forests today is nonsense. Too much has changed. . . ." Although the welfare of India's tribal communities has received little attention from government, basic health care programmes have meant that death rates among most of them have steadily declined. However, birth rates have not, and consequently their numbers have increased dramatically in many areas. Gujjars are polygamous and many families have fifteen to twenty members. Attempts to translocate the gujjars within the national park to areas outside have been half-hearted, poorly executed and strongly resisted. At present some 5,000 gujjars still remain within the national park. "It's a very sensitive issue," concluded Dr Johnsingh. "Unfortunately, we need rules to control how people behave in the forests, and they must apply to the tribals just like everybody else. At present the gujjar population is rapidly going up; they don't want to stall-feed their buffaloes, and they want lots of them. . . . The system simply can't stand this sort of pressure."

The lion-tailed macaque is one of many species whose survival is threatened by habitat fragmentation.

Habitat fragmentation now poses one of the most significant threats to a whole range of creatures in India. Its most conspicuous victim in and around Rajaji is the Asian elephant, whose numbers have been declining across the breadth of the sub-continent for many years. At least 40,000 elephants were captured or killed during the past century, but it has been the loss and degradation of their forest habitat which has contributed most to the species' decline. Of the four separate populations in India, the largest, amounting to perhaps 12,000 beasts, is found in the moist forests of the north-east; the southern states of Karnataka, Kerala and Tamil Nadu support a population of 6,000–7,000 elephants, and there are over 2,000 elephants in the central states of Orissa and Bihar. The smallest of the four populations, and probably the most endangered, is found in the Shivalik hills and the *terai* of Uttar Pradesh. There the elephants' strongholds are the forests of Rajaji and Corbett national parks, which, though separated by a strip of unprotected land, should be treated as a single conservation unit. "You've got to take them together," stresses Dr Johnsingh, "and we want to use the elephant to promote this idea. It's big, it's very visible, and it moves."

Elephants traditionally make seasonal migrations across their home range in search of food and water, but over the past half-century, the migration paths used by elephants in Uttar Pradesh have been much reduced, and sometimes completely blocked, by human activities. Within Rajaji national park the links between the eastern and western portions have been almost entirely severed. A power channel nine miles long was constructed in the 1970s along the east bank of the Ganges, and a resettlement programme for refugees, together with various industrial developments, turned much of the west bank into a

no-go area. As a consequence the elephant population has been split in two, 200 animals being crammed into the smaller, eastern portion of the park and 100 into the west. Small, isolated populations of animals (and humans) are subject to all the genetic defects inherent in in-breeding. For that reason alone it is important that corridors should be maintained to allow some individuals, and especially bull elephants, to move from one half of the park to the other. Confining a population to one small area and restricting its traditional migrations also puts great pressure on the forest habitat. Dr Johnsingh's team has found that bull elephants only cross from one side of the park to the other at night now, using a bridge across the power channel and four islands in the Ganges. There are real fears that if the vegetation on the islands disappears – and tree felling and grazing have already led to its degradation – the elephants will no longer make the journey along this corridor.

Dr Johnsingh's colleagues at the Wildlife Institute have found that habitat fragmentation threatens many of India's mammals. Dr Renée Borges, for example has spent much time studying Malabar giant squirrels in the Western Ghats. "One of the things I've found", she explains, "is that the squirrels won't travel long distances on the ground; they need a continuous canopy to move around. In fact, the giant squirrel is an excellent indicator species for mature, closed canopy forest." Unfortunately, such forests face many pressures – conversion to agricultural land, logging, overgrazing, to name but three – and the loss and fragmentation of their habitat has meant that the Malabar giant squirrel is now classified as an endangered species. The grizzled giant squirrel of south India and Sri Lanka and the pied giant squirrel, which is found in the forests of the north-east, also face an uncertain future for the same reasons.

*Aftermath of a forest fire in Bandipur national park, Karnataka.
This was probably the work of villagers aggrieved at the area's
conservation status.*

Another endangered species which has been studied by the Wildlife Institute is the Nilgiri langur. There are probably no more than 5,000 of these shy, handsome creatures left in the world, and they are all confined to the forests of the Western Ghats. Over the past century 60 per cent of these forests have been lost, and much of what survives is found in isolated patches. "Fragmentation is a chronic problem," according to Dr Ajith Kumar, who has been studying the langur. "There's very little continuous forest left, with a few exceptions like Silent Valley and Calicut Forest and a thin strip on a very steep scarp running 130 miles along the Western Ghats in Karnataka. There aren't many threats to these big forests, but they only support 20–30 per cent of the langurs. The rest are living in small isolated populations in small scattered patches of forest. They seldom travel from one patch to another and I think their future is very

doubtful. It's just a question of time before many of these small patches of forest disappear." The Nilgiri langur and the Malabar giant squirrel are two species among the many hundreds whose genetic health, and future survival, is threatened by the fragmentation of their habitat.

Violence towards nature has reached its apogee in and around two of India's most celebrated national parks, Manas and Kaziranga. These are found in the Brahmaputra Valley in Assam, one of the seven states which together occupy the politically turbulent triangle of land wedged between Bangladesh, Bhutan, Burma and China. Well over a third of this region is still clothed in dense forest, but it is rapidly shrinking; large chunks have been felled to make way for tea plantations, though the greatest despoilers today are the plywood and paper industries. Kaziranga is dominated by low-lying swamps, semi-evergreen forest and lush grassland; Manas nestles against the Bhutan hills and is scenically the more dramatic of the two. Between them they harbour a large portion of the region's fabulously diverse fauna and flora, and in recognition of their importance they have been declared world heritage sites by UNESCO. Manas is home to more endangered species than any other park in India. The pygmy hog and hispid hare are found only here and in the neighbouring Barnadi wildlife sanctuary, and a fifth of the world's population of the rare Bengal florican lives in Manas. The park is one of the last strongholds of wild buffalo and it contains populations of elephant, gaur and swamp deer. A 1988 census put the number of one-horned rhinoceroses at eighty; however, Kaziranga, with 1,100, is far more important for this endangered species. Both parks also support thriving populations of tiger.

Assam has long been troubled by political unrest, with members of the Bodo tribe, which constitutes approximately a third of the population, becoming increasingly militant in their calls for a separate state. Some of the grievances of the Bodo are genuine. They have seen their forests plundered by the timber and pulp industries and their land appropriated to make way for coal mines and tea estates. In short, their needs and rights, like those of so many of India's tribal peoples, have been studiously ignored by those in power. Until recently, Bodo agitation was confined to cities and towns; sadly, it has now spilled into the countryside. The full horror of it was documented in *Sanctuary* magazine by Goutam Narayan, a researcher with the Bombay Natural History Society:

In the intervening months between the first full-scale assault on Manas by the Bodos in mid-February 1989, much blood has been spilt as brother has fought brother in a vicious war which has brought sorrow and heartache to all of Assam. . . . Militants, armed with sophisticated weapons, have driven away the forest protection force, leaving the jungle open to all takers. Predictably, poachers were quick to take advantage and years of protection is being wiped out before our very eyes.

The militants set fire to many of the forest guard huts, destroyed bridges and terrorized the park staff. They demanded that the government close all its offices in the area and Manas became one of their training camps. "Here the writ of the gun rules supreme," wrote Narayan, who believed that the agitation was being financed, in part at least, by the profits from poaching. "The Bodos," he suggested, "appear to be fighting for no more than what they

By 1908, hunting and poaching had reduced Kaziranga's rhino population to ten or so animals; following excellent conservation measures, their population climbed back to over 1,000 by the 1980s. But poaching is again on the increase – seventeen rhinos were killed in 1991.

consider their fair share of the booty to be earned by converting Manas' natural wealth into cash." Kaziranga also has its problems. In 1991, seventeen rhinos were killed by poachers and six poachers were killed by forest guards. On the international market, a kilo of rhino horn can fetch up to £9,000. Little wonder, then, that some people are prepared to risk their lives for it, though it is the middle men – the besuited wheeler-dealers in Delhi, Bangkok and Hong Kong – who take the lion's share of the profits.

It is hard to say exactly what impact poaching has on wildlife populations within India's parks and sanctuaries, although there is plenty of evidence to suggest that it continues on a significant scale in many parts of the country. The southern population of Asian elephants has certainly suffered from the activities of poachers, who slay the tusked males and leave the females. In Mudamalai, there are said to be six females for each male and the ratio may be even more skewed in other heavily poached areas. The principal villain in the south is a sandalwood smuggler and ivory poacher called Veerappan. He is wanted by the police for an estimated forty murders, for killing at least 500 elephants and for the felling and smuggling of £6 million-worth of sandalwood. Veerappan and his gang have been on the run for several years and poaching activity is said to have declined. Towards the end of 1991 the divisional forest officer in charge of the task force set up by the Karnataka government to apprehend Veerappan was murdered. Mr P. Srinavas had evidently been tricked by the poacher into visiting his hide-out. I met several conservationists who sneered at the government's efforts to catch Veerappan. This struck me as grossly unfair. The Forest Department and police are hampered, in many instances, by a lack of manpower and equipment.

Many of the threats to parks and sanctuaries – poaching, grazing, wood smuggling, the lopping of trees for fodder and fuel – are opportunist, in the sense that they stem from the initiative of individuals rather than the design of government ministries or industrial corporations. However, it is the activities of the latter which pose the greatest threat to some protected areas. Sariska national park, in southern Rajasthan, provides one of the clearest examples of the way in which industry and government, in this case the state government of Rajasthan, have conspired to wreck a national park. During the last century, Sariska was the hunting reserve of the maharajahs of nearby Alwar. It was declared a sanctuary in 1955; in 1979 it came under the auspices of Project Tiger and three years later it became a national park. Sariska encompasses 300 square miles of dry, hilly country and within its boundaries is one of the last sizeable remnants of the forest which once stretched the length of the Aravalli Hills. The forest is home to tiger, leopard and jungle cat as well as a good population of sambar, chital, nilgai and porcupine. The presence of tigers, and the park's proximity to Jaipur and Delhi, have made it a popular tourist attraction. However, if its ruination at the hands of mining interests continues much longer, there will be little left for tourists to see: the number of tigers in the park fell from forty-five in the mid-1980s to nineteen by 1988. Other animals have suffered too.

Sariska is rich in marble, dolomite and limestone, and as long ago as the 1960s the state government was happy to give private companies licenses to mine the stone. Mining within national parks violates Rajasthan's Forest Conservation Act, but this has been of no concern to the state's mining department, which now earns an estimated £1·1 million a year from licensed workings. During the past six years more than 300 licences have been issued for mines within the park. Despite protests from central government, Rajasthan's chief ministers have always backed the mining contractors, and indeed many of the mines are owned by politicians. So far about one-fifth of the park, some 60 square miles, has been destroyed or severely damaged by mining activity, which has also had a drastic effect on the water table.

The villagers of Sariska have suffered alongside the wildlife, and midway through the 1980s a group called Tarun Bharat Sangh was set up to encourage the wiser use of local resources. Among its many achievements – the group's activities have ranged from health education to tree-planting – has been the creation of some 200 *johads*, the traditional water-harvesting bunds once common throughout Rajasthan. During the past few years mining activities have caused many *johads* to run dry, and in 1991 Tarun Bharat Sangh laid the issue before the Supreme Court. The court found in favour of Tarun Bharat Sangh and ordered all mining in the park to cease by the end of the year. If anything, mining activity has increased since then. Rajinder Singh, secretary of Tarun Bharat Sangh, was beaten up together with several colleagues by a group of mine owners shortly after the Supreme Court judgement. The ringleader was sentenced to seven days' imprisonment and a fine of 500 rupees (£10).

NATURE BITES BACK

Newspaper headlines like "Man-eaters of Garhwal shed their fear" and "Leopard mauls five in Orissa" occur almost weekly in the Indian press. It is impossible to say exactly how many people are killed

"Lion killing the farmer's wife who had eloped with a prince."
Modern version of a seventeenth-century Moghul painting
by Husain Va'iz Kashisi.

each year by wild animals, but a survey carried out at the end of the 1980s by the Indian Institute of Public Administration hints at the scale of the problem. Many parks and sanctuaries failed to respond to the questionnaire, but those that did, some fifty in all, reported 629 attacks on humans, 485 of which were fatal, during the period 1979–84. There were 221 tiger attacks, 189 taking place in and around the Sunderbans national park in West Bengal; 68 bear attacks, most in Madhya Pradesh; 56 elephant attacks; and 21 attacks by leopards, or panthers as they are more commonly known. One person had the misfortune of being killed by a blue bull or nilgai. The key problem area apart from the Sunderbans was Dudhwa national park in Uttar Pradesh, where there were 119 attacks. The number of animal attacks for Gir lion sanctuary was put at twenty-five, or five a year; the annual toll today is far greater, and indeed many parts of India have witnessed a steady rise in man-eating and man-killing. To some extent, this reflects the success of conservation policy: as predator populations have increased, so have attacks on humans. It is also a function of human population growth; wild animals which find their habitat invaded by people increasingly take matters into their own mouths. The specific tragedies of lives lost are all too apparent, but these man–animal conflicts are tragic for conservation too, for without the goodwill and help of those who live beside protected areas, their wildlife is doomed.

When I met Mr R. Radcliffe, hunter-turned-conservationist in the Nilgiris, he pointed out that wildlife managers seldom saw things from the villagers' point of view: "You can't expect them to live with tigers and elephants threatening their lives and their crops. In just one night an elephant can destroy everything in a field. In theory the villagers are supposed to get compensation if a tiger kills a cow or a buffalo, but the system often fails." The government, argued Mr Radcliffe, expected villagers to live with tigers and leopards in their midst, yet these creatures "would not be allowed one minute of

*Butter-making in a village near Gir lion sanctuary. The
Maldharis' economy is based on their cattle.*

life if found in the parks of New Delhi or Bombay or in the grounds of Buckingham Palace or Hyde Park in London!"

The Asiatic lion never reached quite as far west as London, but in medieval times it ranged across a vast area between Turkey and the Bay of Bengal. Being creatures of open savannah, the lions were easy prey for trophy hunters and farmers who considered them a pest. By 1893 there were just thirty-one Asiatic lions in the world, all of them in the Gir forest of southwest Gujarat. Nine years later there were twenty, and the species seemed destined for extinction.

A scene of deceptive serenity; attackss on humans by lions have risen sharply in recent times (overleaf).

Fortunately, the Nawab of Junagadh, the owner of Gir forest hunting preserve, decided to protect the lions and their numbers soon began to rise. By 1920 the lion population was fifty-strong, and by the time of independence there were well over 200 animals. Lion hunting was finally banned in 1955 and ten years later the government created the 488 square-mile Gir wildlife sanctuary, expelling from the core zone of 100 square miles the *maldhari* pastoralists and their buffalo. There was a small decline in the lion population during the 1970s, since when it has risen to almost 300. No one disputes that this has been a great success story, but the costs in terms of human lives lost have become unacceptably high. Between 1978 and 1988 eight people were killed by lions and sixty-five injured, whereas in the two and a half year period which followed there were twenty deaths and ninety-nine injuries. Of those killed, almost half were eaten or partially devoured. The number of livestock killed by lions also rose, from 743 in 1987–88 to 1,706 by 1989–1990. As one researcher remarked, the villagers and pastoralists took a dim view of all this: "Typically, it was suggested that if the Government of India is keen on protecting the lions, it should take the lion population to Delhi and that government officials may feel less strongly inclined towards saving the beast should they have to face the nightly fear of lions close to home." Lions are not the only problem in Gir. Leopards are also numerous, and between May 1988 and March 1991 they killed four people and injured 69.

A young ecologist called Ravi Chellam has spent four years studying the lions of Gir and he has delved deep into the complexities of man–animal conflicts. "The forests at Gir can only accommodate a certain number of lions," he said when I met him at the Wildlife Institute of India. "There are now too many

of them – they go into the villages in search of goats and buffaloes and other animals. The villagers try to defend their stock, or sometimes they bump into the lions by chance and the lions attack them. It's no good tranquillizing the lions and releasing them again in the core zone – that's been the Forest Department policy so far. Lions and leopards that attack people should either be shot or taken to a zoo."

Many of the villagers interviewed by Chellam attributed the increase in lion attacks, most of which occurred around the edge of the national park, to the expulsion of the *maldhari* families and the ban on livestock grazing in the core zone. The logic goes as follows: lions have always preyed on domestic stock, and shifting the *maldharis* and their animals out of the park has encouraged the lions to follow them; in doing so, they have been brought into more frequent contact with villagers on the park's periphery. However, Chellam points out that the *maldharis* were removed in the mid-1970s, and he suggests that the sudden increase in lion attacks was more probably triggered by the severe droughts of 1986 and 1987. Fodder became so scarce in those years that many wealthy villagers transported their herds to other parts of the state where supplies were plentiful. The poor were unable to adopt such a policy and many of their livestock starved. The availability of livestock as prey was further reduced as villagers increased the levels of protection they afforded their herds. Chellam believes that the scarcity of food caused many lions to become bolder and more aggressive. Villagers reported lions jumping compound walls and in some cases breaking into houses to get at the livestock. According to Chellam, "It is but a step further to realize that such aggressive searching for prey would undoubtedly lead to increased chances of attacks on humans."

Losing one's life, or a relative, to a dangerous carnivore is nothing new for the fishermen, wood-cutters and honey-gatherers living in or near the Sunderbans national park, which encompasses over 1,000 square miles of magnificent mangrove swamp in the flat deltaland in the mouth of the Ganges. West Bengal's department of tourism suggests that "Contrary to popular belief all Sunderbans' tigers are not man-eaters. Only 5 per cent have been found guilty." Five per cent of 300 – the present number of tigers in the reserve – is fifteen, which, as far as those who live there are concerned, is fifteen too many. The villages which suffer most are those on the edge of the core zone; Arampur is now known as "tiger widow village", having lost over 150 men to tigers in recent times. A scientist dispatched to the Sunderbans in the 1970s to study the man-eating problem suggested that drinking the brackish water, with its high salt content, might cause physiological changes which induced the desire to prey on humans. The director of Project Tiger dismissed the idea; if it were true that the water caused behavioural aberations, then one would expect it to affect more than the 3–5 per cent that prey on humans. However, the tigers of the Sunderbans constitute a special case, being almost a separate sub-species adapted to a semi-aquatic life.

Dudhwa national park became notorious for its tigers in the early 1980s. Dominated by the finest example of sal forest in India, Dudhwa was declared a wildlife sanctuary in 1965 and a national park twelve years later. Among the many interests opposed to the establishment of the sanctuary was the Forest Department, which at the time was more impressed by the sal's economic potential than by the wildlife it harboured. Dudhwa owes its existence, and to some extent its survival, to the remarkable talents of one man, Billy Arjan Singh, whose "Tiger Haven" on the southern edge of the park has proved a great attraction to tourists and visiting biologists. In his book *Tiger! Tiger!*, Singh discussed man-eating: "Now, as I write at the beginning of 1984, the number of people killed by tigers in Kheri is over 110 and is moving inexorably upwards. The outbreak has caused widespread panic and distress, not least because it is quite unlike anything that India has known before." Singh believes that primitive hunters must have constituted part of the tiger's diet, along with deer, pig and other creatures. When *Homo sapiens* settled into an agricultural way of life, took to wearing clothes, standing erect, talking loudly and living outside the forest, tigers shunned his company and vice versa; there was room enough for humans and tigers to co-exist peaceably. In recent times, however, humans have pushed further and further into the forests, converting them to agricultural uses and degrading them by logging and slash-and-burn agriculture, thus depriving the tigers of their ancestral homes. Hence the emergence of a pheno-menon which died out tens of centuries ago: man-eating and man-killing. Jim Corbett believed that many man-eaters were forced to adopt the habit as infirmity or old age prevented them from success-fully hunting more agile prey. This alone, says Singh, is insufficient explanation for the present man-eating phenomenon. "Nature, the final authority," wrote Singh, "has at last rebelled against the liberties which humans have been taking in the assaults on the environment, and struck back in spectacular fashion."

Imagine flying over Calcutta's Eden Gardens during an international cricket match; you will see an oasis of green surrounded by a dense, heaving mass of humanity. Dudhwa is like this: an ever-expanding human population pressing in upon the forest, and

*A poster outside Corbett national park: "Reigned terror from
1918 to 1926. Killed over 300 people – shot by Jim Corbett on
1 May 1926".*

agricultural crops now run right up to the very boundaries of the park. As far as the tigers are concerned, sugar cane, which is widely grown here, is little different from a stand of reeds or tall grass: a pleasant, cool place in which to rest. The tigers frequently see farmers and their wives coming into the fields, perhaps to hoe weeds or answer a call of nature, and before long they lose all fear of humans. In the cane fields man-eating becomes inevitable, just as it does when humans wander too far within the park. Since the practice of allowing villagers to collect firewood and thatch grass – *nikasi* – was

banned in 1985, the incidence of man-eating has declined dramatically. However, all is not well. Villagers – understandably, many would say – have taken to slaughtering tigers whenever they can, either by poisoning them or shooting them, and farmers and loggers continue to chip away at the forests in and around Dudhwa.

Many states pay no compensation for loss of life or livestock and in those that do, the payments vary wildly. Some, for example, pay as little as 200 rupees (about £4) to the family of someone killed by a wild animal; at the other end of the scale, a family might

*Vast flocks of geese spend the winter months in Keoladeo Ghana
national park.*

*Painted storks are among the most conspicuous and noisy
of the many colonial species which nest in Keoladeo Ghana
national park.*

get 10,000 rupees (or about £200), which is more than many people would earn in a year. Ravi Chellam found that the villagers in Gir were very critical of the Gujarat State Forest Department, whose staff were alleged to show little concern for those who suffered the attacks of lions and leopards. They complained that the compensation system was so cumbersome that many did not even bother to claim for their losses.

Throughout India there are many areas where villagers have become deeply hostile to the whole idea of conservation, and the poor relationship between the officials in charge of parks and sanctuaries and those who live and farm beside them is a cause for much concern. One in six of the protected areas responding to the survey mentioned earlier in this chapter reported confrontations between the park authorities and villagers. The worst clash in recent times took place in the bird sanctuary of Keoladeo Ghana at Bharatpur. The events which led up to it are instructive, as they show that the exclusion of human activity is not always in the best interest of wildlife.

Keoladeo Ghana national park, or Bharatpur as it is also known, has had a remarkable history. Arriving by train (Bharatpur is an hour from Agra) the visitor climbs on to a cycle-rickshaw and progresses slowly through the dusty backstreets towards the soggy, green paradise which lies a mile to the south of the town. The visitor dismounts to pay a modest entrance fee at the park gates, then continues, if he or she has any sense, half a mile or so to the Forest Lodge, where simple accommodation and good food can be had within listening distance of one of the world's finest heronries. Had a visitor to Bharatpur made a similar journey 150 years ago he would have found a scrubby depression of land, seasonally enlivened by ephemeral ponds of water following the

monsoons. These ponds used to attract migratory duck and geese in the winter months and the royal family of Bharatpur took advantage of their presence by shooting them. However, towards the end of the last century the Maharajah of Bharatpur decided to establish a permanent wetland here and a series of canals and dams were built. Before long Bharatpur had become one of India's most productive hunting reserves. In 1956 it was declared a wildlife sanctuary.

I doubt whether there is any other place in the world where such a variety of birds can be so easily observed. The park covers a mere 11 square miles, approximately a third of which is wetland, and you can cycle around the main paths in a day or so. We arrived late one afternoon and within half an hour of leaving the Forest Lodge had seen jackal, mongoose, sambar, wild boar and at least eighty species of birds out of the 350 which regularly nest or visit here. Vast numbers of egret, stork, cormorant, spoonbill, ibis and heron had turned a babul wood into a raucous

*Scores of migratory species must make the perilous journey across
the Himalaya.*

and smelly slum. Jacana, pond heron and white-breasted waterhen stalked silently over the lily pads while whiskered tern and pied kingfisher plunged into open water in search of fish and eels. In the dry scrub beyond the water's edge there were mynahs, drongos, shrikes, bee-eaters and parakeets. The geese and ducks which fly south from the northern breeding grounds to spend the winter here had just begun to trickle in, but it was still too early for Bharatpur's most famous visitor, the Siberian crane.

Siberian cranes were frequent visitors to Bharatpur in the days before the Maharajah developed it into a hunting preserve. Regular shoots, however, drove these handsome birds elsewhere and it was not until 1960, several years after *shikar* had ceased, that they returned again. Three cranes arrived that year, but by 1964–5 over 200 came to winter here. Over the years their numbers have dwindled and in 1990–1 only ten cranes came to Bharatpur. There are several factors which appear to have led to the decline. A breeding pair of cranes only raises one chick each year, and though they are formidable adversaries – adults stand well over four feet tall – the young sometimes fall prey in the nest to skuas, gulls and dogs. Once the winter begins to draw in, members of the western race of Siberian crane leave the northern breeding grounds to make the long journey south to the only two places where they are known to over-winter: Feredunkenar in Iran and Bharatpur in India. The 4,000-mile long flight to India is perilous, and every year some of the cranes perish in Afghanistan and Pakistan, where they continue to be shot despite those countries' efforts to protect them. The cranes' feeding requirements are highly specialized: they are predominantly vegetarian and they favour the rhizomes and tubers of a small number of aquatic plants. When the cranes came back to Bharatpur in the 1960s and 1970s, they found a restaurant much to their liking. Unfortunately, it is no longer the gourmet establishment it once was.

The Forest Department, whose thinking no doubt was swayed by the prevailing belief that humans should be excluded from national parks, decided to evict villagers' livestock from the park in 1982. This move backfired in more ways than one. It is true that buffalo may have been rather too numerous before the grazing ban, but they did at least suppress the growth of weeds such as water-hyacinth and restrict the spread of certain invasive sedges. Once the buffalo were excluded, weeds ran rampant and the Siberian cranes' food plants declined. Scientists now believe that the western race of Siberian cranes may number no more than twenty and its present plight is due, in part at least, to the exclusion of buffalo from Bharatpur. Several years ago, villagers decided to drive their livestock back into the national park: they were met by armed police and seven of them were killed for doing no more than exercising what they consider to be a traditional right.

RETHINKING CONSERVATION

Government officials are well aware of the need for some sort of *rapprochement* between wildlife and its guardians on the one hand, and the villagers and pastoralists whom they so frequently antagonize on the other. "In our enthusiasm", R. L. Singh, the director of Project Tiger, had told me, "we ignored some of the side effects of conservation policy. We stopped grazing and firewood collection in many forests and millions of tribals and local people were put to disadvantage. That's why we've launched an ecodevelopment programme."

*India's national parks are increasingly threatened by poaching,
encroachment and fire-raising. Fighting the fires in Bandipur
national park, Spring 1992.*

Getting a wood-cutter to see reason in a south Indian national park. Words have failed, so a forest guard resorts to hurling stones at the miscreant. It all ended amicably enough (above).

A forest guard poachers in south India (below).

"Ecodevelopment" has become the catchphrase of the 1990s for India's conservationists. Much to its credit, the Government of India seems to be taking the issue seriously: according to Mr Singh, it intends to spend 72 crore rupees (around £16 million) on the second phase of Project Tiger, the main purpose of which is to resolve the conflicts within and around reserves and provide help to the tribals and villagers. Ecodevelopment programmes have already begun around Gir lion sanctuary. "We've got to help meet the demands of the villagers," explained the warden, Shyamal Tikader, as we bumped through the teak scrubland near his headquarters. A jackal trotted down the rutted track ahead of us and a herd of spotted deer browsed in the high grass. "What we have to do is show the villagers that there are tangible benefits from conservation, that if we look after the forests at Gir, they'll have adequate supplies of water, fodder and fuel. If we don't conserve the forests, this area will turn into an arid wasteland."

The ecodevelopment at Gir has concentrated on the provision of energy; by September 1991, 156 gobar gas plants had been set up in ten villages around the sanctuary. Half the finance had come from Gujarat Agro-Industries, a quarter from the Forest Department and a quarter from the villagers themselves. Gobar gas plants turn animal dung into cooking gas and provide an alternative to fuelwood. "We've worked out that these plants will save 1,200 kilograms of wood a day," explained Mr Tikader; "That's 438 quintals a year or about 5,000 trees." In order to get the dung, the villagers must stall-feed their livestock, which, of course, takes grazing pressure off the forest. The use of gas rather than wood also helps the women. "Now they don't have to spend hours away from home searching for fuelwood," said Mr Tikader. "They can see more of

*Back from the brink; good conservation work has saved the great
Indian bustard from extinction.*

their children and they can concentrate on activities like embroidery, which generates cash." The warden had no doubt that the survival of Gir depended on the goodwill and cooperation of the villagers.

Ranthambhore national park in southern Rajasthan has witnessed the most comprehensive ecodevelopment programme to date. There are some sixty villages around the park with a population of getting on for a quarter of a million people, a good number of whom were pushed out of their old homes under a resettlement policy which removed fourteen villages from the park. For hundreds of years the area encompassed by the park – a superb mosaic of forests, grasslands, lakes and streams – had provided local people with the stuff of life: fodder, firewood, thatching grass, fresh water. Removing these from within the park's core zone has now become a criminal offence and villagers have been forced to rely on the slender resources available outside. Inevitably, the environment has begun to suffer. The Ranthambhore Foundation was established in the late 1980s by Valmik Thapar, author of three books on the tigers of Ranthambhore, to help improve the quality of life of the villagers living round the national park. The Foundation has established a primary health service which has brought simple medicare, an immunization programme, family planning and health education to tens of thousands of people. A dairy and animal husbandry programme, with a strong emphasis on stall-feeding, will reduce livestock activity round the park, and the Foundation is also trying to raise milk yields by improving the quality of the livestock. With the help of the Foundation, traditional arts and crafts have been revived in some villages and this has generated extra income, especially for women. A seed bank set up by the Foundation enabled villagers to plant 24,000 saplings in 1991, and 750 children are regularly involved in ecodevelopment projects.

Non-governmental organizations like the Ranthambhore Foundation have a key role to play in protecting the Indian environment. They may lack financial clout, but they have proved time and again, as we shall see in the final chapter, that dedication and enthusiasm, combined with a good dose of bloody-mindedness and a refusal to be intimidated, often count for more than a healthy bank balance. Ecodevelopment programmes in and around national parks will obviously rely heavily on the support, political and financial, of central and state governments, but park authorities need the help of non-governmental agencies too; it will often be easier for them to gain the confidence of tribals and villagers than for the park officials, whom many rural dwellers view as adversaries.

Ecodevelopment programmes are being launched in some unlikely places. Despite the violence of the Bodo agitation, college students in Assam are working on a project set up by the World Wide Fund for Nature (India) to help the villagers living beside Manas national park. "We realize that we've got to address the social issues first," explained WWF's Devika Sircar. "Once the villagers have better health care, clean water and improved educational facilities, it'll be much easier to encourage them to care for the wildlife in the forest." Like many of India's young conservationists, Devika joined one of WWF's nature clubs while she was still at school. "Once you have some interaction with villagers, you realize just how hard up they are. A while ago we came across some villagers killing barbets. They weren't poachers, they were simply taking the birds because they needed food. It's easy to be angry, but we have to see things from their point of view. . . . That's why we tell our

Marsh muggers have been successfully bred in captivity at the Madras Crocodile Bank and released into the wild.

nature clubs not to sermonize." The Manas project had only just begun when I met Devika. "At the moment", she explained, "the students are going round the villages and carrying out socio-economic surveys. Once we have found out what the village people need, we can start practical work. We'll set up education programmes and help to build gobar gas plants. . . . We've got to convince the villagers that the sanctuary is not just for wildlife – it's for them as well."

The steadily worsening relationship between humans and elephants – around 300 people are killed each year – was one of the factors which prompted the Government of India to set up Project Elephant, with a budget of 19 crore rupees (approximately £4 million) over the next five years. Under Project Elephant scientists will identify the corridors along which the animals migrate and work out ways to protect them. In some cases entire villages may have to be moved. "But we won't repeat the mistakes of Project Tiger," asserted R. L. Singh. "Ecodevelopment will be an important component of our work for the elephant." It is too early to say whether Project Elephant will help to save India's most noble herbivore, but at least the elephant is being afforded a degree of protection which other endangered creatures such as the Nilgiri langur and the Malabar giant squirrel, also bedevilled by habitat loss, simply cannot even hope for.

The idea that man and nature can coexist lies at the heart of the 'biosphere reserve' concept. This has been with us since the mid-1970s and India is one of over sixty countries which have set up biosphere reserves. By 1991 there were thirteen such reserves encompassing a great range of habitats, from the swamps of the Sunderbans to the Himalayan peaks of Nanda Devi, from the Thar Desert in Rajasthan to the coral reefs of the Gulf of Mannar. Each biosphere reserve has a core zone in which wildlife is strictly protected and no human activity is countenanced. Surrounding these untrammelled areas is a buffer zone where there is a modicum of human activity.

The villagers and the authorities in charge of the biosphere reserve must practise and promote – in the awful parlance of today – "sustainable development". The biosphere concept was first championed by UNESCO and its purpose is to establish a network of reserves which will protect the entire spectrum of ecosystems around the world. Many conservationists in India believe the biosphere approach could help resolve conflicts between wildlife and humans. So far, progress has been distressingly slow.

Chapter Six

COASTAL TRAUMAS

The modern traveller nearly always reaches India by air, to be greeted by long ribbons of tarmac, pernickety officialdom, aggressive taxi drivers and the dispiriting suburbs of Delhi, or maybe Bombay or Madras. One envies the European travellers of a century or less ago, who made a leisurely entry by boat to Bombay, were disgorged along with their trunks and hunting gear near the Gateway to India, and from there had but a few paces to walk to the cool foyer of the Taj Hotel. That was a grand and satisfying introduction to the Orient, but better still must have been the sea approach made by the tens of thousands of explorers, missionaries and traders of earlier times. It is said that Arab spice traders found their way to the Malabar coast, which encompasses the present day state of Kerala, by following the shoals of oil sardines which migrate down the western shoreline. One can picture them still, these tough, turbaned, sword-wielding men, as they guided their vessels into the larger harbours to take on a cargo of cardamom and pepper, or splashed barefoot through shallower waters, their nostrils filled with the enticing scent of woodsmoke and palms, their spirits lifted by the sight of the Western Ghats rising above the dense greenery of the coastal forests.

Fishing is a perilous occupation; one of Kerala's traditional mango-log kattumarams *heads out to sea.*

One of the earliest accounts of India's coastal wildlife is to be found in *The Travels of Marco Polo*, first published at the end of the thirteenth century, although Edward Gibbon must have come across earlier documents, as he wrote in *The Decline and Fall of the Roman Empire* of the large fleets which visited Malabar each year to buy silk, spices and a variety of wild animals, which were later slain in the amphitheatres of Rome. Marco Polo was especially taken by the Malabar coast around the fishing port of Quilon: "The country produces a diversity of beasts different from those of all the rest of the world," he wrote. "There are black lions with no other visible colour or mark. There are parrots of many kinds. . . . Then there are peacocks of another sort than ours and much bigger and handsomer, and hens too that are unlike ours. What more need I say? Everything there is different from what it is with us and excels both in size and beauty."

Much has changed since then, but of beauty, superficially at least, there is still no shortage. Indeed, there is scarcely a single vista on Kerala's 370-mile coastline which would not grace the covers of a tourist brochure advertising a tropical paradise. Mile after mile of glistening sand is fringed by groves of feathery palms on one side and the deep blue sea on the other. On nearly every beach in southern Kerala you will see fishermen setting out in their mango-log *kattumarams* and tight-breasted, slim-waisted women with glistening black hair and upright backs heading landward with the morning's catch balanced on their heads. I imagine that sights such as these greeted Marco Polo wherever he landed. Perhaps life appeared as idyllic then as it does now; if so, this is an illusion of long-standing. Spend a little time on the beaches here and you will soon see why the eye at first deceives.

I began my journey along the coast a few miles north of the state capital, Trivandrum. We pulled up a few minutes' walk from the sea and parked in the shade of a three-quarters built church; the stations of the cross were already in place but otherwise the tall nave was bare of ornament. We headed through the palms to the beach; butter-coloured sands stretched as far as the eye could see. A few *kattumarams* bobbed on a gentle swell some way out, but the greatest concentration of fishermen was to be found on the beach. Thirty sinewy, bare-chested men pulled at two thick ropes attached to a large seine net which had been set half a mile or so from the shore. It took an hour of intense, muscle-aching work to pull the net in; the fruit of this labour was a small haul of anchovies. My companion, an English fish biologist, suggested that the catch might be worth 40 rupees, or about 1 rupee for each fishermen, insufficient to buy a cup of *chai* in the local cafe. We headed further north and walked down to the beach again, this time following the waste outlet of a titanium factory: the sand had been scorched grey by the acid effluent and the sea streaked brown with pollution. No one was fishing here so we drove south again. We stopped at one village where several *kattumarams* sped through the surf on to the deeply shelved shore, whence their occupants rushed their catch to the auctioneers on the beach. One fisherman got 40 rupees for his catch; another only 25.

Kerala's 30 million inhabitants are among the best educated, least fecund, healthiest, most politically conscious and independent-minded in India, but the fishing community, which is predominantly Christian, is conspicuously poor compared to the rest of the population: most of the villages we had passed through were overcrowded and malodorous, but nothing quite prepared me for

Hauling a small shark ashore on the coast of Orissa.

Vizhinjam, a fishing village a mile to the west of Kovalam Beach, one of southern India's most popular tourist resorts. At Vizhinjam's westerly end a monumental mosque with rocket-like minarets towers above the palms; the opposite side of the bay is dominated by a large Catholic church set in spacious grounds and commanding a fine view of the beach slums. These are occupied by several thousand fishing families and they are as unpleasant as virtually any you will see in Bombay or Calcutta, the mud

Chinese fishing-nets in Cochin; these ingenious devices are said to have been introduced to the Malabar coast by the courtiers of Kubla Khan.

hovels separated from one another by pathways which reek of decay and diesel fuel. There is no sanitation system – the beach is Vizhinjam's toilet – and drinking water is drawn from a pitifully small number of standpipes.

For thousands of years the people of the Malabar coast have made a living from the sea; life was always simple and tough, but there were enough fish to satisfy the needs of all who fished. Over the last two decades all this has changed. Kerala's fishing industry provides a classic example of greed conquering prudence; of the frailty of natural resources when a few choose to exploit them to excess. The story is a complicated one and I heard it from various mouths: from John Fernandez and Aleyamma Vijayan at the Programme for Community Organization (PCO); from Aleyamma's husband, the General Secretary of the Kerala Independent Fishworkers' Federation (KIFF); and from V. Vivekanandan, the chief executive of the South Indian Federation of Fishermen Societies (SIFFS). These three organizations – a Christian pressure group, a trade union and an umbrella group for cooperatives – were dedicated to bettering the lot of Kerala's fisherfolk and they had been largely responsible for what little progress had been made in tackling the injustices which in recent years have made poor fishermen even poorer.

The fishing communities of southern India employ a remarkable range of techniques to tap the plentiful supplies of fish and shellfish. Around the attractive port of Cochin you will still see scores of cantilevered Chinese fishing nets, which are said to have been introduced by the courtiers of Kubla Khan; a little further south, round Alleppey, large fifteen-man canoes, or *thanguralloms*, are favoured; while the fishermen further south have traditionally used the smaller *kattumarams*. Before the 1960s there were no

mechanized boats in Kerala's waters, but the seeds of change had already been sown as long ago as 1952 with the establishment of the Indo-Norwegian Project (INP). For years the INP had only a tiny influence; its early attempts to motorize traditional craft were abandoned, and its impact was only felt when it began experimental bottom-trawling for prawns. "In the old days," explained Vivekanandan of SIFFS, "the fishermen didn't make much money from prawns. Unless they were very fresh, people tended to get stomach upsets, so instead of eating them, the prawns were often used as fertiliser for the palm groves." But merchants discovered that there was a good market abroad for frozen prawns and by 1961 a tonne would sell for 4,000 rupees in the USA and double that in Japan, vastly more than fresh fish fetched locally, which was about 150–200 rupees a tonne.

Thus began the scramble for "pink gold", and a new class of absentee trawler-owner appeared on the scene. "Most of the owners are businessmen with other interests," explained Vijayan, the union leader. "They simply move in and out of whatever happens to be profitable. For example, in the 1970s, wage demands by workers in Tamil Nadu's cashew plantations encouraged plantation owners to sell up and buy trawlers in Kerala instead." Killings were made in good years and several entrepreneurs – including, astonishingly, the leader of Kerala's Revolutionary Communist Party – acquired upwards of a dozen boats. In 1971, the total catch in Kerala stood at 445,000 tonnes, 90 per cent of which was taken by artisanal (traditional) fishermen; four years later the catch was down to 420,000 tonnes, by which time the small mechanised fleet of trawlers accounted for 43 per cent of the fish taken. By 1980 the total catch had declined to 280,000 tonnes and the artisanal

Many of Kerala's fishing communities live in picturesque squalor. The introduction of a capital-intensive trawler fleet has simply made matters worse for most fisherfolk.

sector took just over half; in other words 100,000 or more traditional fishermen had seen their catch decline from 398,000 tonnes to 144,000 tonnes in just ten years. The only people who gained were the owners of the 3,500 or so trawlers operating out of Cochin, Neendarken and one or two other large ports. Before trawlers appeared on the scene artisanal fishermen caught 30,000–35,000 tonnes of prawns a year; by 1974 the catch had risen to 83,000 tonnes, 80 per cent of which was taken by trawlers. The prawn catch is again down to around 30,000 tonnes a year. "So, despite the introduction of all the modern technology," explained Vivekanandan, "the catch hasn't increased; rather, it's been transferred from one sector to another, from the poor to the rich."

The artisanal fishermen have reacted to the trawler threat in a variety of ways. At one time, they took to capturing the trawlers at sea, removing their crews and setting the vessels alight. They have also resorted, often with the help of the union, to "agitation": blocking harbours with canoes; blocking city roads (and once Trivandrum airport); marching through the streets; mounting hunger strikes. Kerala has generally been ruled by left-wing or communist governments that have tolerated the agitations; however, when the Congress (I) party was in power in 1984, Vijayan and his fellow unionists were badly beaten up by the police.

From an environmental point of view, the artisanal fishermens' other response to the trawler threat – motorization, as it is clumsily known – could prove disastrous. Initially a few fishermen bought 5hp motors to help them get to the fishing grounds more rapidly and thus compete with the trawlers. Then some began buying 45hp motors, and today some have 250hp motors fitted to their boats. Now half the traditional craft are motorized and three quarters of

*The voracious appetite of trawlers such as these is taking
food from the mouths of traditional fisherfolk.*

*A trawler's haul: a basketful of glistening crabs awaits auction at
Panaji harbour, Goa.*

the fishermen work on them; this has inevitably created tension within the artisanal sector because the large motorized craft have a catching power not dissimilar to the trawlers they so despise. In their quest to modernize, many fishermen have fallen heavily into debt to money lenders, and the social problems in places like Vizhinjam become ever more acute. According to Aleyamma Vijayan of PCO, alcoholism is rife and wife-beating common. Men and women spend much of their time away from their homes, doing the best they can to make money; consequently, the children of the fisherfolk are ill-fed, illiterate and ill-kempt.

The human suffering is plain for all to see, but it is somewhat harder to determine the nature and severity of the environmental damage along the coast. Nevertheless there is plenty of evidence to show that bottom-trawling is devastating the shallow water reefs which are particularly important for fish life – as places for spawning, feeding and shelter – and for the traditional pole-and-line fishermen. Bottom-trawling also rips up the sea bed around the reefs, killing all manner of invertebrate life and devastating spawning-grounds. John Fernandez of PCO calls it "deforestation under the sea" and he has been helping villagers to create artificial reefs to attract fish back into areas denuded by trawlers. "The impact of overfishing can't be seen as explicitly as deforestation on land," says Fernandez, "but there's little doubt that fish stocks are declining, and the level of fish catches certainly doesn't reflect the great increase in effort which has been made over the last two decades." From a low of around a quarter of a million tonnes, the annual fish catch has recently risen again to the 400,000 tonne mark. Many attribute this to the recent ban on trawling during the monsoons, a ban which has persistently been demanded by the artisanal

sector. "But the ban's been very half-hearted," says Fernandez, "and we really need the government to go along with the findings of all the scientific commissions we've had. They say the fishery can only support 1,000 or so trawlers, rather than the 3,500 now operating." Vivekanandan at SIFFS agrees that the trawler fleet will have to be reduced if fish stocks are to remain healthy, but he's brave enough to suggest that there are also too many artisanal fishermen – perhaps 130,000 today, compared to 115,000 in 1980.

In fact, there are several other threats to the coastal ecosystem which may prove as significant as overfishing, although in evaluating them one tends to stumble around on the borderline between fact and conjecture. "Kerala gets plenty of fresh water with its two monsoons a year," says John Fernandez, "but deforestation in the Western Ghats and the damming of many of the state's forty-four rivers is altering not just the flow of water, but the quality of the brackish water where the fresh water meets the sea. This is

Over four fifths of India's mangroves are to be found in the Sunderbans, a steamy mosaic of swampland at the mouth of the River Ganges.

bound to affect the spawning-grounds of prawns and many fish." His colleague Aleyamma Vijayan feels that the reclamation of Kerala's backwaters to make way for rice paddies and other crops is also having a deleterious effect on spawning; pollution, too, whether from factories such as the one producing titanium near Trivandrum, or from the villages and towns along the coast, is also a major worry.

In Search of Wild India is not so much a natural history as an exploration of the links between man and nature, which are exemplified, on the coast, by the dependence of many fishing communities on the survival of mangrove swamps. Once upon a time Kerala had 7,000 hectares of mangroves; today less than a tenth survives. This is a sad loss, both for the diverse agglomeration of invertebrates, fish, amphibians, reptiles and birds which depend for their existence on mangroves, and for the fishermen who in turn depend on some of these creatures for their livelihoods. But it is a small tragedy compared to the one taking place further up the west coast, in Maharashtra and Gujarat.

If any ecosystem can be described as bizarre it is the mangrove swamp. Anyone viewing a swamp for the first time could be forgiven for thinking it a simple world, verging on the dull. Mangrove leaves are a lustreless green, the trees often have a scrubby appearance and the swamps seem to lack the great diversity of species which one associates with terrestrial forests in the tropics. But mangrove swamps are much more than nature's shock absorbers, protecting friable coasts from the constant battering of the seas: they support a rich and often peculiar fauna and flora. Somewhere in the region of 350,000 hectares of mangroves remain around the Indian coast. Over four-fifths are found in the Sunderbans of West Bengal and the Andaman and Nicobar Islands, but

there are important concentrations in Orissa (5,000 hectares), Maharashtra (20,000 hectares) and in Gujarat's Gulf of Kachchh (20,000 hectares). There are 59 species of mangrove in India, 54 of which occur on the east coast and 32 on the west. The precise nature of mangrove swamp varies from place to place, depending on a whole variety of factors such as salinity, the slope of the coast, water temperature and the intensity of the monsoons. A rich mangrove swamp will support well over 100 species of plant, a score of crabs, maybe a dozen species of prawn, 30-odd species of fish and 100 or more birds.

This is the tale of two islands: Ajad and Chusna, the former the only inhabited island in the Gulf of Kachchh, the latter one of the few whose mangroves have remained unscathed. The film crew and I arrived at Ajad late one evening in the company of Rishad Pravez, the marine biologist who had taken me to Salaya to fix up the hire of a trawler some five months previously, and Smita Krishnan, a former colleague of Rishad's and now a biology teacher in Bombay. We stumbled around in the dark, pitched tents somewhat ineptly and devoured the fish and prawn biryani cooked by the fishermen who had brought us here. That we had arrived at all struck us as something of a miracle. Countless hours had been devoted over the past few months to extracting all the necessary permissions from the various bureaucracies and organizations who had an administrative or proprietorial interest in the Gulf, but at the last moment the Forest Department, which is responsible for the Gulf of Kachchh marine national park, demanded that we obtain a written all-clear from the Indian Navy. Our request was passed from one commanding officer in Gujarat to another, then to Naval Intelligence in Bombay and finally to the

Ajad's cattle have made rather too much of a meal of the island's mangroves; elsewhere in the Gulf of Kachchh mangroves are being felled at an alarming rate to supply fuelwood, timber and camel fodder.

Fifty years ago this corner of Ajad supported a dense mangrove forest. "The place of trees" has become a place of death (top).

The destruction of mangroves has led to a dramatic rise in siltation in the Gulf of Kachchh. Ajad's coral reef has been reduced to an almost lifeless wasteland with little more than the odd lump of brain coral and a few sea anemones (bottom).

Ministry of Defence in Delhi. By the time assent was given, we had been kicking our heels for a week in Bombay. We had the distinct impression that the Forest Department was not especially keen on us filming wildlife in the Gulf, an impression reinforced by the attitude of the official who eventually allowed us to proceed. On no account, he said, should we film the cutting of mangroves or any of the pollution spilling into the sea from the Gulf's coastal industries. By the time we reached Salaya, our trawler-owner had grown tired of waiting for us and despatched his eleven vessels to the fishing grounds. However, we hired the services of the admirable Adam Moosa Bhayar and for a week his trawler – alluringly painted in pastel shades of pink and green – became our mobile home as well as the means for procuring sustenance.

Ajad was having a busy week. A party of Harijans – "the children of God", as Gandhi had called the Untouchables – had arrived to gather up the bones of the cattle which had recently died in an epidemic, causing the island's bovine population to plunge from forty to less than ten; and a barber from the mainland had come too, not, it transpired, to cut hair, but to relieve a number of young boys of their foreskins. Ajad, explained Rishad, meant "the place of trees", which it once had been. Nowadays, it is one of the more barren places in India, having been afflicted by years of maltreatment by humans and a succession of droughts. In years when the monsoons do bring rain, the islanders, who number around 170, sow pearl millet and sorghum, but recently the rains had failed, the cultivated fields had remained fallow, and the twenty-one families had been forced to rely solely on fishing for their survival.

At one time much of this small island had been rimmed by mangrove swamps. There had been a

Mitha Chusna is a paradise for birds; egrets, herons, darters and storks roost on the rocky shore.

particularly fine stand, some of the older islanders told us, in the bay beside our camp, but the mangroves had been cleared to make way for a bauxite mine. Mining had long since ceased, and all that remained was a lifeless, lunar landscape. No longer restrained by the roots of mangroves, the tides stripped the mud away and carted it out to sea to be deposited on a coral reef so smothered with sediment that it no longer deserved the name. Here and there little knobs of live hard coral poked through the silt, and in some rock pools there were soft corals too. A few orange and black brittle stars and multi-coloured sea slugs browsed over the silt, but sea anenomes were the only creatures which seemed to thrive. We had intended to film this reef when the tide was in, but the sediment rendered the water so murky that we abandoned the idea.

Ajad is by no means entirely devoid of wildlife. A few small patches of mangrove have survived and although these have been much degraded by cutting and grazing, they harbour a reasonable population of breeding birds and attract many migrants. The crew spent a day and a half filming here, and, this being winter, got the sort of footage you might expect from a British estuary, with sizeable flocks of migratory waders feeding tirelessly on the invertebrate harvest of the mudflats. There were large flocks of curlew, little stint and dunlin, and smaller numbers of ruff, black-winged stilt, crab plover, Caspian tern, painted stork, grey heron, reef heron and little egret, but we realized just how modest Ajad's birdlife was when we reached the island of Chusna, which, unlike Ajad, truly deserved a name such as "the place of trees". Chusna is made up of two halves: Khara Chusna, meaning "salty suck", is separated at high tide by a thin channel of water from Mitha Chusna, or "sweet suck".

We arrived an hour or so before sunset and waded on to Mitha Chusna, a small lump of land submerged beneath a magnificent canopy of mangroves, some of the older trees towering thirty feet above the sand. This was truly a paradise for birds. Dozens of darters had begun nesting in the mangroves and within a month they would be joined by the egrets, herons and storks which, as the sun sank and the sea washed across the vast expanses of intertidal mudflats, congregated in dense, noisy flocks on the rocky outcrops which fringed the island. The incoming tide also drove the waders off the mudflats and dunlin, knot and little stint whirled above the island in flocks a thousand-strong; less numerous but more musical were curlew, redshank and sandpiper.

At night we slept beside the small *dargah*, or Muslim shrine, on Khara Chusna. Captain Adam was entrusted by the local fishing communities with the care of the shrine – it looked like a small mosque – and he slept alongside us on the sand outside the *dargah*'s entrance. The week before there had been a big festival: according to Adam, eighty people had slept here for four nights, and five thousand for a night or two. Lavatorial facilities being non-existent, we felt the presence of the pilgrims still, and on the rocks behind the *dargah* were the feet and entrails of the thirty-six goats which had been slaughtered to mark the anniversary of the death of the saint who was buried here. That Chusna's mangroves still flourished was entirely a reflection of the island's sanctity. I asked Adam what would happen to someone who tried to cut wood here. "He'd suffer for it," he replied. "Bad things would happen to him within a couple of weeks. He wouldn't be able to sleep well, or he'd have bad dreams; perhaps his boat would sink, or his fishing nets would split. . . ." Chusna, he conceded, was one of the few places in the Gulf where the

mangrove was not suffering from human demands. He refused to point the finger of blame at the fishing community, for obvious reasons, but all the studies carried out by Rishad, Smita and their colleagues indicate that it is the fishermen who do most of the damage. Indeed the fishing communities of just three settlements, including Adam's home of Salaya, cut some 10,000 tonnes of mangrove each year, and if the destruction continues at the present rate there will be next to none left in ten years' time. It is hard to predict precisely what effect this will have on the Gulf's fisheries but it will be considerable. Mangroves act as nurseries for prawns and many species of fish; their loss will be the fishermen's too. The late Professor R. M. Naik, whom I had met at Saurashtra University shortly before his death, had told me that while some of the older fishermen were concerned about the future, the younger generation seemed oblivious to the deleterious impact their activities were having on the Gulf's ecology.

In 1982 the government established the 500-square mile Gulf of Kachchh marine national park. There is little which the poorly paid (and often poorly educated) forest guards can do to stop the fishermen cutting the mangroves, and it is doubtful, in any case, whether some of the more senior officials are seriously committed to protecting the park's wildlife. One can take some comfort from the fact that coral reefs in the Gulf are no longer mined to supply raw materials for the cement industry, but the destruction of the mangroves is slowly leading to their being smothered to death. The discharge of industrial pollutants is also on the increase, especially along the south coast between Jamnagar and Dwarka.

Towards the end of 1991, the Saurashtra University team produced a lengthy report on the Gulf in which it made a series of recommendations, aimed mostly

A quiet smoke after a long night out; the trawler heads back to Salaya (below).

(Overleaf.) The man-made saltings near Jamnagar, in the Gulf of Kachchh, attract many different species of waterbird, including the spectacularly lovely greater and lesser flamingo.

at the national park authority. There is an urgent need, it argues, for better education, better health care, improved sanitation and a serious family planning effort. Many of the Gulf's environmental problems stem from ignorance and poverty. All mangrove cutting should cease, as should the harvesting of mangrove leaves, a practice sanctioned by the state government during drought years; a forestry programme should be established to provide the coastal communities with their fuel and fodder needs, and the Forest Department should restore degraded mangrove forests and plant new ones. The report deplores the use of fishing nets whose mesh size leads to the harvesting of juveniles, and calls for the banning of DDT, a pesticide used by some fishermen to attract fish. Certain areas, especially those support-

ing good mangrove vegetation and marine life, should be closed to all forms of exploitation, including fishing.

Policing large expanses of ocean is a notoriously tricky business at the best of times; the task in the Gulf of Kachchh is made all the more difficult by the lack of resources, both financial and human, at the disposal of the park authority. Those responsible for the park's welfare may plead this as a mitigating circumstance, but one cannot help feeling that they could be doing much more to protect the Gulf's wildlife. At the time of our visit, some five months after the publication of the report, they had failed to make any response to its findings or recommendations. Unless they do something soon, the Gulf of Kachchh will be turned into an aqueous desert.

Several hundred thousand olive Ridley turtles nest on the beaches of Orissa each spring; the effort proves too much for some.

The wildlife of India is often tantalizingly discreet; of course, you can easily witness the large gatherings of waterfowl and cranes during the winter months at Bharatpur and in many other wetlands, but seeing tigers, or leopards, or even wild elephants, is no simple matter, even if you visit areas where they are to be found in plenty. Likewise, the chances of the casual visitor coming across any of the five species of sea turtle which nest along the Indian coast are fairly remote. Yet India's olive Ridley turtles are responsible for one of the most awesome spectacles in the natural world. The beaches which play host to the annual *arribada*, or arrival, of nesting olive Ridleys are well off the beaten track, and in any case the turtles nearly always come ashore under cover of darkness.

Every year around the end of January and early February vast numbers of female turtles emerge from the Bay of Bengal to clamber clumsily on to the ten-mile long beach which fringes the national park of Bhitar Kanika in the state of Orissa. Each turtle excavates a pit, lays 100–130 eggs, buries them, then heads back to the sea. Around fifty days later, the eggs hatch and millions of tiny turtles rush swiftly seaward to toss themselves into the incoming surf. In many years there is a second *arribada*, and the outgoing young must run the gauntlet of the incoming adults, which squash countless numbers as they crawl like winged tanks to the upper beach. The number of turtles nesting along the Orissa coast varies from one year to another. In 1983 the *arribada* was 800,000-strong; but 250,000–300,000 is the norm, and on odd occasions only 10,000 or so have turned up.

At the lower end of the evolutionary spectrum, nature tends to be profligate with her progeny: for every 100 turtle eggs, perhaps ten give rise to hatchlings which make it to the sea, and just one to a hatchling which will return, five years later, after a 1,500-mile journey, to breed for the first time on the beach where it was born and where the majority of its siblings died. Turtle eggs and their hatchlings make excellent fodder for jackals, dogs, wild boar and even crabs. The sea is also full of enemies: while the young are gobbled up by carnivorous fish of modest proportions, or grabbed by frigate birds or gulls, the adults are easy meat for killer whales, sharks and other large fish. The natural hazards have always been here, but people have now emerged as major predators and their activities over the past fifty years have meant that all of India's sea turtles are now classified as endangered. Once upon a time olive Ridleys nested in great numbers along the entire east coast of India. A generation ago there were said to be 100 nests along every kilometre of the Coromandel coast to the south of Madras; now there are perhaps ten nests, and in some places none at all.

I can think of little to say about Madras, either in favour or against, but I can be rather more positive about some of its inhabitants. Those I met – many of whom were involved in the conservation of reptiles –

were delightful, unfailingly helpful and as memorable as the city was dull. I prefaced my perambulations along the coast with a visit to Preston Ahimaz, a young man of great charm and vivacity who runs the Tamil Nadu branch of the World Wide Fund for Nature (WWF). We talked of many things – among them, the threat to Mudamalai and the Nilgiris – but we began with olive Ridley turtles. "The robbing of eggs is a big problem," explained Preston. "If a dog or a jackal finds a nest, it'll eat half the eggs and leave the rest; when the poarchers find a nest they take all the eggs." In village markets the eggs sell for 15–20 paisa each (there are 100 paisa to one rupee), which is about a quarter of the price of hens' eggs. For the poor they provide a good source of cheap protein, and until not long ago, turtle egg soup was served as a delicacy in fancy hotels.

Preston was one of many people who had helped established turtle hatcheries on the coast to the south of Madras. Romulus Whitaker, an American settled in India and a herpetologist of international stature, is credited with making the first move to save the turtles, and the work continues today under the auspices of the Students' Sea Turtle Conservation Network. As it happened, neither of the young men who took me down the coast to see the students' hatchery were students: Dipankar Ghosh ran a variety of educational projects and a PR company, and Shebbar Sheerazi worked for ICI India. Dipankar felt that social changes along the coast had worked against the turtles: "In the old days there were only fisherfolk here, but now there are lots of outsiders who have been brought up in the cities and know nothing about wildlife. Some of these people even kill the hatchlings just for the fun of it."

At Neelangarai beach we met the partially disabled fisherman who spent the nesting season looking after the hatchery. This consisted of a neat thatched hut, where he slept, and a small plot of fenced-off sand which was home to the eggs collected by the students. "About twenty of us regularly walk this beach," said Shebbar, his arms encompassing a broad stretch of sand to the north and south. "When we see turtle tracks we dig up the nests and bring the eggs here. This year we've brought in the eggs of 205 nests." The eggs – say, 120 for each nest – had been reburied at the hatchery and some hatchlings had already been discharged to the ocean. "We reckon on sixty to seventy eggs hatching for each nest," explained Shebbar, "so that'll mean we'll release around 14,000 baby turtles this year."

In the early days of the turtle work (for several years the Department of Environment and Forests also ran hatcheries) the local fisherfolk viewed the conservationists with animosity and disdain. "They found it hard to believe we weren't doing it for money," said Dipankar as we released a bucket-load of newly hatched olive Ridleys into the frothy sea. "But now they respect what we are doing. We have an unwritten agreement that if the poachers get to a nest first, they take the eggs; if we do, we get them." But, I queried, how can you tell if all this work has made any difference to the turtle population? "Well, we can't," admitted Shebbar, "but if we hadn't picked up the 205 nests this year, the poachers would have found and taken at least four-fifths of them. So we must be making a difference." Needless to say, the threats to the seaborn turtles remain: adults are still taken by trawlers, inadvertently or otherwise, as well as by their natural predators, and in some areas they are still killed for their meat, leather and shells.

Unfortunately for the turtles, the Indian coastline is being built up rapidly. "Ten years ago", recalls Preston Ahimaz, "you could walk along the five

*Mass tourism threatens not just the coastal wildlife of Goa, but
the welfare of the locals too. Many villagers have to go without
drinking water because it is diverted to the tourist hotels.*

miles of coast south of Madras and you'd only see
one or two lights at night. Now it's lit up all the way
– you're never out of sight of street lamps or houses."
These unnatural illuminations confuse the turtles,
which are attracted after laying or hatching to the
brightest part of the sky, which is generally above the
sea. Now many head towards the lights inland to be
crushed on the roads. The problem is even more
acute around the tourist resorts of Goa on the west
coast. In 1981 Mrs Indira Gandhi, who was then
Prime Minister, outlawed all construction projects
within 500 metres of the high-tide mark unless they
were sanctioned by the Ministry of Environment.
This was an enlightened measure aimed at safeguard-
ing beaches, mangrove swamps and, among other
things, the nesting sites of turtles. However, the limit
was later reduced from 500 to 200 metres, and in Goa
many developers ignore it altogether: the tourist
industry is now threatening to build more than
seventy new hotels along a coastline which is already
suffering from over-development. Many hotels
floodlight their beaches at night to satisfy the
hedonistic desires of their western clients, and the

turtles, whether adult or young, head towards the
lights, making them easy prey for jackals, dogs and
poachers. Recently, the Ministry of Tourism – not
noted for its environmental awareness – mooted the
idea of establishing resorts on the Andaman Islands
and the Lakshadweeps, two outstanding regions for
marine wildlife. To many in power, tourist dollars
and pounds count for much more than the well-being
of dugongs and turtles.

This chapter has concerned itself with a range of
threats to India's coastal wildlife. In a sense it has
been a story of individuals against nature; of men and
women being driven, often by poverty, sometimes
by cupidity, to act in ways which destroy or damage
coastal resources. Frequently one sympathizes: were
you or I to find ourselves in the shoes of a poor
fisherman, wouldn't we cut mangroves and collect
turtle eggs if by doing so it alleviated our poverty, in
however meagre a way? Yes, of course we would.
But there are others – the trawler owners of Kerala,
for example, and the hoteliers of Goa – whose
activities one can only deplore. Few would claim that
natural resources should not be exploited; they
should be, but in such a way that they are available
not just for those who live today but to the millions
who will populate the Indian coastline centuries
hence. India's foremost turtle expert, Satish Bhaskar,
has suggested that one of the main objectives of
research at the Orissa nesting sites must be to
forestall the egg losses which result from beach
erosion and "to eventually make turtle eggs, which
are a valuable protein resource, available for human
consumption, without affecting natural turtle populations". The turtles, the fish, the prawns, the
mangroves, the mudflats – all, if managed with care
and good sense, could help sustain the human
populations who live beside them.

A window on to the past? Goa as it used to be.

Chapter Seven

FIGHTING FOR A GREEN FUTURE

The dawn sun cast an opaque light across the dusty streets as we drove through Indore's shabby, small-town suburbs and headed south into good rolling countryside. My driver predicted that we would cover the sixty miles to the Narmada River in a couple of hours; we would reach Barwani, forty miles or so downstream, in time for lunch. Travel in India is a capricious business, frequently glorious, but at times indescribably gruesome. Within an hour we had passed five accidents involving overladen lorries; at least one had resulted in the death of the driver. Then one of our tyres split like a ripe fig and we slewed across the path of an oncoming lorry, narrowly missing it but making intimate acquaintance with a shallow ditch. On close inspection, I found the other tyres to be as bald as vultures and after lengthy remonstrations I abandoned my car and driver, to be picked up soon after by a schoolteacher from the village of Thikri. It was hard work for his moped, but it was good to feel the fresh wind and smell the dry earth. Before long we were crossing the broad Narmada. On the far side a large gathering of women sat in silence next to the road. A young boy had been almost torn in two by a lorry; my chauffeur slowed in order to observe him the better, then we sped on our way. He was a cultured, intelligent man, and entirely unruffled by what he had seen. In much of India death is a commonplace affair; in the Narmada Valley, it may become even more so in the near future.

India's forests provide much more than timber. A girl in a
village near Dharwad, Karnataka, makes plates from
the leaves of the muttala tree.

151

Jawaharlal Nehru, India's first prime minister after independence, used to talk of big development projects as the "temples of the future"; he was especially enamoured of dams, which he believed would supply the country with vast quantities of electricity, irrigate tens of millions of acres of hitherto unproductive countryside and help transform India into a land of milk and honey. In 1987, after two decades of talk and planning, the Narmada Valley Development Project finally got under way with funding from the World Bank; it involves the building of 30 major dams, 135 medium dams and 3,000 minor dams. The Narmada Project, which will be the greatest project of its type ever undertaken, has sparked off one of India's most potent environmental protests. For many it is a matter of life and death; quite simply, they are prepared to drown for what they believe.

It was mid-afternoon by the time I reached Barwani and I immediately made my way to the office of the Narmada Bachao Andolan, the organization spearheading opposition to the dams. The office occupied two small rooms above a shop; a couple of youths, lounging on a mattress with their exercise books, explained through gestures and sign language that the people I had hoped to talk to were all absent. However, I was led to a nearby shop and introduced to a slender, quietly spoken young man who offered to take me to see Baba Amte, the father figure of the Narmada protest movement. We climbed on to his motorbike and juddered our way down a dirt track, through fertile fields of cotton and maize, to a small "encroachment" overlooking the river. On the way there we passed a large police camp. "They're very hard on us," said my companion. "They frequently harass people coming to see Baba." He risked a beating by bringing me here, and when I met him later that evening, back at the bus station in Barwani (where he presented me with a little notebook and a propelling pencil), he simply said, "It is my duty; you are our guest." The bravery of those who speak out against the Narmada dams, and against other projects which threaten India's people and wildlife, never ceased to astonish me.

Unfortunately, I arrived at an inopportune time: Baba Amte was surrounded by a dozen people who had just made a two-day journey from Anandwan, the celebrated settlement for lepers and the blind established by Baba some thirty years previously. Nevertheless, I was immediately made welcome. Baba was now approaching eighty, yet he had the physique of a man thirty years his junior; he was muscular, bow-legged and strikingly handsome, with a hawkish nose set in a broad face bordered by silver hair and dense sideburns. A spinal problem prevents him from sitting; so he either stands or lies down. His health may be shaky – he invited me at one point to feel the hard knob of a pace-maker under the skin of his chest – but he exudes courage and passion. "I shall die here," he said bluntly. "When the waters rise and engulf this bit of land, I shall drown. I shall not move – or they'll have to carry me out in a

*Dissent spills into the cities – an anti-Narmada protest in
downtown Bombay.*

coffin." Later, as the blood-orange sun sank over the
denuded hills to the west, Baba's son Vikas, a doctor
at Anandwan, showed me round the plots of
vegetables and herbs which sustained Baba, his three
helpers and his wife (I think the lack of salt was all
that prevented them from being totally self-sufficient).
"Holding our Annual General Meeting here is an
excuse to see my father," Vikas explained. "He's not
really interested in the past. This is all that matters to
him now." A blue bus pulled up on the river bank a
couple of hundred yards downstream from where we

stood and thirteen police climbed out and stared
towards us. "They've set up that halogen lamp to
upset Baba," said Vikas. "It shines into his hut all
night long." On one occasion they even brought
loudspeakers here and bombarded him with music
for twenty-four hours. They did the same thing
when he led a protest march to the Gujarat border
earlier in the year; on that occasion, the state's chief
minister had sanctioned the harassment. "If the
government is so sure of its case for the dams," said
Baba, "why do they encourage the police brutality

against us?" Vikas suggested that Baba was "one of the most hated men in India: the government, politicians, big business – they all hate him."

Baba Amte is among the most prominent of those who have put themselves in the front line of the Narmada struggle. Many others operate from a somewhat safer distance – Indore, Bhopal, Bombay, New Delhi – but they too play a vital role. They have tirelessly questioned the assumptions which have driven the state to commission the dams; they have brought pressure to bear on the World Bank and foreign aid agencies (sometimes successfully – the Japanese, for example, have withdrawn their support); and they have ensured that the deeds of Baba and his friends remain in the public eye. The issues raised by the Narmada affair transcend the mundane business of irrigation and power supply: "The World Bank and the government say they want to develop India," said ex-minister Om Prakesh Rawal when I met him at his home in Indore. "But develop for whom? And at what cost? Hundreds of thousands of people, most of them tribals, will lose their homes and forests because of these dams. They're going to be thrown out like garbage! What we are talking about here is not just lost forests, submerged temples, drowned wildlife – we're talking about the right to life."

A few weeks later, in the more salubrious surroundings of New Delhi, N. D. Jayal, the director of INTACH, the Indian National Trust for Art and Cultural Heritage, expressed his fears thus: "I had fifteen years in government before Mrs Indira Gandhi invited me to set up INTACH. I was a rebel. I saw that many things were wrong, that big dams always caused terrible damage to nature and people. On the one hand government is saying we should conserve land, conserve wildlife, yet on the other, it's sponsoring destruction. It's time we worked out our priorities.

Do we want western models of development – more cars, more consumption, more wealth for the rich, less for the poor? Or do we want to alleviate poverty and improve life in the villages? To promote a style of development where resources are evenly shared? At present, the ruling élite thinks only in terms of western-style development. They are urban-based; they know nothing about the environment. They're more worried about raising money to get re-elected than they are about the future!"

"Our slogan", Mr Rawal told me, "is *Koi nahin hatega – Bandh nahin banega*: 'Nobody will move – the dam will not be built'." Well, this all sounds a bit dated now. Construction of the Sardar Sarover in Gujarat is well under way and the waters are beginning to rise behind a concrete curtain some 140 metres high and 1,200 metres long. The government and the scheme's financial backers believe that the Narmada Project will solve Gujarat's perennial problem of drought. The waters of the Sardar Sarover, according to official forecasts, will irrigate 1·8 million hectares of land (6,950 square miles) and supply 3·5 billion litres of drinking water each day. In addition to this, the dam is set to produce 1,450 megawatts of hydro-electric power. The cost of the whole project is put at £3·5 billion and the completion date hovers around 2010.

Millions of words, in a variety of languages, have been devoted to analysing the pros and cons of the Narmada Project and anyone wishing to immerse themselves in the subject will find some pointers in the bibliography. Those unfamiliar with the "big dams debate" – it has preoccupied environmentalists and aid experts for over a decade – must bear two things in mind. First, the proponents of big dams always exaggerate the benefits, skate over the disadvantages, underestimate the cost and inflate the life

The massive workings of the Sardar Sarover Project in Gujarat; 250 villages will go under water and over 100,000 people will be displaced (below).

Shaping their own destiny: children working at the Narmada Sagar Project, Madhya Pradesh (right).

expectancy of their schemes. Second, their protagonists have a tendency to make things sound even gloomier than they really are. All the same, it soon becomes apparent to even the casual observer of India's dam-building history that it has been a shambles. Indeed, the former prime minister Rajiv Gandhi had the following to say in 1986: "The situation today is that, since 1951, 246 big surface irrigation projects have been initiated. Only 65 of these have been completed and 181 are still under construction. We need some definite thrusts from the projects that we started after 1970. Perhaps we can safely say that almost no benefit has come to the people from these projects. For sixteen years we have poured money out. The people have got nothing back, no irrigation, no water, no increase in production, no help in their daily life."

The state governments which stand to benefit from the Narmada Project talk of dams as though they were some sort of celestial elixir which prolongs and enhances life. Opponents suggest that there is nothing life-giving about the project, that the opposite is true. The Sardar Sarover alone will lead to the submergence of 250 villages and 40,000 hectares of land, at least a third of which is dense primary forest. According to the government, at least 100,000 people, 60,000 of them tribals, will lose their land, their homes and consequently their livelihoods. Admittedly, there are plans to provide the "oustees" with land elsewhere, but India's resettlement record following the building of other dams has been appalling. Kisan Mehta, one of the elder statesmen of India's environmental movement, argues that the government figure for the oustees is, in any case, an underestimate. "They only count the people who would actually go under water if they stayed put," he told me when I met him in Bombay. "But what about those who will be displaced by all the roads, the construction work and the canals – after all, they're talking in terms of 70,000 kilometres of canals? We've calculated that the number of oustees will be nearer 300,000 than 100,000."

The Sardar Sarover dam has been described as the "life-line" for arid Gujarat, yet over two thirds of the drought-prone regions within the state will not receive a single drop of the Narmada's water. "Saurashtra is one of the areas worst hit by water shortages," said Mehta, "but there's little chance of water getting there. You can't transfer water 450 kilometres in temperatures of 45 °C without most of it evaporating. Instead, what we shall see is water going to those areas which already have enough. And when it gets there it'll be used to irrigate land to grow cash crops such as tobacco for people like you!"

According to Mehta, no dam in India has ever performed as predicted. "Look at the Ukai dam – that was supposed to irrigate 200,000 hectares of land. In fact, the dam submerged 60,000 hectares and it only supplies water for 30,000. So it's led to a 30,000-hectare loss." The Tawa Dam in Madhya Pradesh also submerged a much greater area than its waters have succeeded in irrigating. I was told in Indore that many of the Tawa oustees now scratch a living collecting bomb cases in an artillery range. "Needless to say, they are always getting blown up," said my informant.

One reason why so many of India's dams have failed to perform as predicted is that the engineers have consistently underestimated the rate at which their creations silt up. For example, a dam on the Manjira River in Andhra Pradesh, though just forty years old, had already lost almost two-thirds of its capacity as a result of siltation, which has occurred at a rate sixteen times greater than the engineers predicted. One dam lost a third of its capacity for similar reasons in just two years; another, the Balawadi, has silted up altogether.

So why do the World Bank and other lending institutions agree to fund schemes like the Narmada project? "Well, whatever it says to the contrary," said Mehta, "the World Bank never looked seriously at the environmental and human rights issues. They didn't even make a proper cost–benefit analysis. They simply looked at India's credit-worthiness – we've got a good record of servicing our debts. But increasingly we'll have to run up more debts just to service the ones we have." Heavy borrowing may impoverish India as a nation, but building dams makes many an individual fortune. Once all the vested interests have climbed aboard the dam-building juggernaut, no argument is likely to bring it

*Going nowhere – many grandiose projects like the Dimbhe Dam
in the Western Ghats are abandoned before their completion.*

to a halt – or so it seems, if one looks at the history of the Tehri dam in Uttar Pradesh.

Plans for a dam at Tehri, a small town beside a tributary of the Ganges in the foothills of the Himalaya, date from the time of independence. Some preliminary work was carried out in the 1970s, but it was President Gorbachev's offer of Soviet financial assistance in 1986 which decked the bones of an engineer's dream with concrete flesh. The town of Tehri – which will be submerged along with twenty-odd villages and much fertile farmland – sits a mere ten miles from a boundary between two continental

Moving mountains – Tehri Dam workings form a macabre backdrop to school lessons.

plates; consequently it is a prime candidate for an earthquake, and indeed one devastated the region, flattening villages and causing hundreds of deaths, in the autumn of 1991. Fears about the geological instability of the dam site helped to trigger widespread protest, both in India and abroad, following Gorbachev's offer of financial assistance, and the Government of India set up a working group under the chairmanship of Sunil Kumar Roy to assess the environmental impact of the proposed scheme. In his submission to the Department of Forests and Environment, Roy concluded: "I confess that my experience in this case as chairman has been harrowing and distressing. I have chaired innumerable committees and groups in India, and in other parts of the world. I have never encountered such an unbending dogmatic approach to all issues. . . ." Roy had come up against many people who were determined that the Tehri dam should be built. His committee recommended that the project should not go ahead and the Department of Forests and Environment endorsed its recommendations. The government, however, set up another committee, consisting largely of officials involved in dam-building, and this committee, not surprisingly, suggested that work should proceed. Despite the protests of environmentalists, scientists and the tens of thousands of people whose homes and land will be submerged, the government probably will go ahead with its plan to build the dam. Let us hope that the seismologists are wrong. If the dam, once full, were to be destroyed by an earthquake, the flood waters would devastate the holy cities of Hardwar and Rishikesh and drown tens, or perhaps hundreds of thousands of people. Incidentally, in 1967 the cost of the Tehri dam was put at 126·8 crore rupees; by March 1990 this figure had risen to 4,142 crores.

Villagers drawing water from a coastal well in Kerala.

Environmentalists are frequently criticised, especially by those who disapprove of them, for their negative attitude; they always seem to be opposing things. This is certainly true, but one should no more castigate environmentalists for speaking out against violence to nature than one should Amnesty International for condemning torture. The environmental movement in India is still in its infancy. Some say that it began with a famous speech by Mrs Indira Gandhi at a United Nations conference in Stockholm in 1972; others that it dates from the birth of the Chipko movement, about which more later. But despite their youthfulness, many organizations have rapidly learnt that it is no good denying one form of development without promoting another. The anti-Tehri dam campaigners have suggested that a series of locally controlled, small "run of the river" dams would bring great benefits to the Himalayan villagers (who stand to gain nothing from the big dam) and at the same time ensure the survival of the valley, its villages and its people. Likewise, the Narmada Bachao Andolan has investigated alternatives to the government scheme for the Narmada River. On the power front, it advocates a combination of energy conservation measures and decentralized power generation. As far as water supply is concerned, the Andolan favours the building of a large number of small projects to harvest and conserve the available water resources. When I first heard of these alternatives, I thought they seemed too vague, too insubstantial to amount to anything more than lightweight anti-dam propaganda. I changed my mind once I had spent a week in northern Rajasthan.

During the early 1980s the city of Jodhpur – famous for an article of clothing and a magnificent, honey-coloured fort – suffered a series of acute water shortages. The government was eventually forced to install hundreds of tube wells and hand-pumps and it brought additional supplies of water by pipe and canal from a distance of over 100 miles. Jodhpur sits on the fringe of the Thar Desert, in a region accustomed to drought, and over the centuries the city developed an elaborate system of water-harvesting which, had it not been forsaken, might have saved the government some expense and the inhabitants some hardship. Less than a century ago Jodhpur had over 200 sources of fresh water, including some 50 tanks, or reservoirs, 50 *bawdis*, or step wells, and 70 ordinary wells. The catchment area, which covered 14,000 hectares (54 square miles) of rocky land behind Jodhpur, was criss-crossed with a network of canals which delivered the water to the city.

The architectural magnificence of the city's tanks and wells astounded not only ourselves but our guide, who, though a resident of Jodhpur for thirty years, knew little about his people's erstwhile genius for collecting and conserving water. Wherever we went people who lived beside the tanks came to tell us of their history. The city's most important tank is Ranisar, which was built by the wife of the founder of Jodhpur, Rao Jodharji, in 1500AD. The tank lies inside the fort walls – this gave it protection from poisoning by enemies – and water was lifted into the main body of the fort by means of a Persian wheel, the remains of which can still be seen. Ranisar has an overflow to Padamsar tank, which was traditionally used by people living outside the fort. Water from both the tanks percolated through the rock and was recovered in step wells and tanks at a lower altitude. Many of these are astoundingly beautiful. I recall, in particular, a magnificent two-storey well with Moghul arcades in the blue-painted Brahmin village behind the fort. Another nearby has domed chambers

163

*Most of Jodhpur's traditional step-wells have been filled with
rubbish or allowed to collapse. A few, like this beautiful
example with Moghul arcades, have survived unscathed,
although their waters are somewhat murky (left).*

*In Remembrance of Times Past; women gather water in the
Thar Desert beside a Rajput graveyard (overleaf).*

at either end of the well, one of which housed a
colony of 300 or more bats; a dead monkey floated
on the slimy green water below. A few of Jodhpur's
tanks and wells still provide the citizens with
drinking water, rather more are used for religious
rites, but most have been destroyed or filled to the
brim with rubbish. Dominating the modern town to
the east of the fort are three large tanks, each over 100
yards square. Gulabsagar is especially lovely with its
waters mirroring the massive walls of the fort, but it
is full of filth and algal scum. A man who worked in
the print works beside the tank could remember the
days when the water was clear and potable; not even
a dog would stomach it now. Wherever we went it
was the same story. Most of the tanks and wells had
been left to decay or turned into rubbish dumps, and
in any case the amount of water reaching the city is a
fraction of what it used to be, for four fifths of the
catchment area is now riddled with quarries and the
network of canals has been destroyed. Forty years
ago the plateau was clothed in forest; today there is
scarcely a tree in sight.

"Now that people have piped water," Kisan Mehta
had said in Bombay, "they don't worry about the old
tanks like they used to. In my village the tanks were
cleaned every five years; now nobody bothers and
they've silted up." Mehta believed that it was time to
revive these old systems of water-harvesting and
devise new ones whose impact on the environment
would be benign. And in many arid parts of India,
this is precisely what is happening. A night's journey
north west of Jodhpur by smutty steam train lies the
medieval walled city and trading-post of Jaisalmer,
surrounded by a forlorn desert landscape, home to
the rare great Indian bustard, to desert lark, to flocks
of migratory sand grouse and other creatures adapted
to an environment permanently short of water. If

you head towards the border with Pakistan you will
pass isolated villages constructed mostly out of mud
or stone, and every now and then you will see
women in flowing saris hauling buckets of water
from deep wells. This region went five years without
rain in the late 1980s and in a good year is lucky to get
more than four or five inches. Nevertheless, the
villagers still manage to grow crops and the desert is
illuminated by scattered patches of brilliant green
where earth or stone bunds have helped retain
moisture for a period long enough to grow millet,
wheat, sesame and animal fodder.

One village we visited was entirely devoid of men;
they've gone to that hill over there, explained the
women, pointing into the distance. The men had left
the day before to spend the night singing and praying
in celebration of the birthday of a Muslim saint. We
passed them as they trod wearily homewards with
their camels and musical instruments late that afternoon. On one side of the hill there was a Rajput
cemetery. The graves of warriors killed in battle
were marked by slender stone pillars with beautifully
carved capitals, a bas-relief of Ganesh on one side, of
the warrior on horseback on another, and between
them of the wife or wives who had committed suttee
to avoid falling into the hands of the enemy. Many of
these pillars were five centuries old, yet perfectly
preserved. To stand in this windswept graveyard,
with its memories of the cruel, brave, chivalrous past,
was an experience made more moving still by the
sight of an emerald-green field of wheat rippling
gently in the desert breeze. The man who many
centuries ago first built a bund here and taught the
people of the desert how to harvest the meagre rains
became a saint, revered by both Muslims and Hindus.
He gave life to the desert, and in doing so he provided
the means of survival for future generations.

The old and the new; solar street lighting in a remote village in the Thar desert.

Which brings me back to the questions posed by Om Prakesh Rawal: "The World Bank and the government say they want to develop India. But develop for whom? And at what cost?" The Muslim saint had developed a system of water-harvesting at minimal cost and for the benefit of the local people; the rulers of Jodhpur had created a more sophisticated system, at considerable expense to themselves, but to the great benefit of the city's population. In neither case did the environment suffer; if anything, it was enriched. As long as Jodhpur relied for its water supplies on its tanks and wells, the forests of the catchment area had to be protected, and consequently wildlife flourished. Compare this with the Narmada and Tehri schemes. The beneficiaries will not be the people who occupy the valleys which are to be dammed. In the case of the Narmada, they will be the large farmers of Gujarat, not the poor tribals of Madhya Pradesh, whose forests will be destroyed. And the Tehri Dam will do nothing for the hill people whose homes it usurps; rather it will provide power and drinking water for cities as far away as Delhi, and irrigation water for the farmers of lowland Uttar Pradesh. The only people who are certain to benefit are the dam-builders, the engineers and the usurers.

There used to be – and perhaps there still is – a handwritten "red-alert" poster tacked on to the wall outside the director's office at the Bombay Natural History Society. This had a list of eight life-threatening activities or projects, the first four of which were proposed or part-built dams: the Narmada, the Pooyamkutta in Kerala, the Bodhghat on the Indravati River and the Tehri in the Himalaya. Dam-building projects and their multifarious consequences are spectacular, and the protests which they generate tend to be in a similar vein, full of sound and fury. Deforestation can also be a dramatic operation – especially when it involves the wholesale destruction of forests to make way for dams, industrial estates or pulp mills – but more often than not it is an insidious process, with forested land being incrementally degraded by poor forestry practices, over-grazing, firewood lopping and so forth. India's environmentalists have had little success in preventing the construction of major dams, their sole victory of note being achieved in Kerala, whose Silent Valley was saved from the dam-builders and turned into a national park. The battle to save India's forests is a more complicated affair, and it cannot be assessed by a straightforward "won or lost" analysis. Nevertheless, dozens of organizations, many consisting entirely of villagers, have managed to save their forests from destruction and convince those who care to listen and observe that India could have a green and tolerable future. The best known of these groups is Chipko, a non-violent movement established in the 1970s by villagers in the Garhwal Himalaya.

A leading figure in the Chipko movement is Sunderlal Bahuguna, a slight, bearded man whose appearance matches the Gandhian principles he espouses. In recent years he has been intimately involved with the battle to prevent the building of the Tehri Dam. Following his lengthy hunger strikes in December 1989, and spring 1992, the government agreed to moratoria on construction while it reviewed the project. But to most people, Bahuguna is associated with the struggle to save India's forests. He is not an easy man to track down; at various times during my travels in northern India I enquired after his whereabouts. On one occasion he was walking the length of the River Ganges; on another he was under arrest. However, I did meet him in the mid-

1980s at a United Nations conference on the Himalaya in New York State. Surrounded by geographers, soil scientists, seismologists and aid-workers, he cut a curious and ascetic figure. He complained about the richness of the food and made us all feel slightly ashamed of our carnivorous habits and material needs, which seemed in his presence so gross. Bahuguna gave an emotional speech about Chipko and the fight to save the forests of the Himalaya. He attacked the international lending banks for frequently funding the exploitation of forests and a gentleman from the World Bank made an uneasy reply. To the World Bank, forests are little more than timber crops and their pecuniary value is paramount. To Bahuguna and those who live in and beside them, their bounty includes edible crops such as nuts, berries, roots and fruits, animal fodder in the form of grass and leaves, fibres for thatching and rope, leaf litter for green manure, and of course wood with which to cook. Timber is just one of many forest products, and to the villagers, possibly the least important. The women of Chipko were motivated in their battles against deforestation by more than self-interest, and they recognized the wider importance of forests in one of their early slogans:

What do the Forests bear?
Soil, Water and Pure Air.
Soil, Water and Pure Air.
Are the Basis of Life

Much of India is scarred by deforestation, whose consequences are appalling: stripped of their trees, hills and mountains are transformed into eroded wastelands, rivers dry up, once fertile farmland turns to desert, wildlife disappears.

*Sunderlal Bahuguna has become internationally famous in
environmental circles; he has been an influential proselytiser for
the Chipko women of the Himalaya, and he has led the battle to
stop the building of the Tehri Dam.*

India's villagers and environmentalists are fighting
against a forest policy rooted in another era. For the
colonial rulers, forests were an important source of
raw material. Having stripped their own oak woods
bare, the British turned to India to supply teak for the
building of ships, and in 1803 the forests of Malabar
became the first of many to be brought under state
control. Large quantities of timber were soon required
for the building of the railways and great tracts of
forest were cleared to satisfy the needs of commerce

and war. "The British treated forests as timber
mines," said Mr Rawal in Indore. "But they're not
mines – they are life-support systems for those who
live there." The British saw forest solely as a source
of timber and many aspects of contemporary Indian
forest policy – and, for that matter, World Bank
policy – continue to reflect this narrow utilitarian
point of view.

Madhav Gadgil of the Indian Institute of Science in
Bangalore believes that the root cause of deforestation

*Karnataka's basket weavers have suffered as a result of the
state-sponsored destruction of bamboo forest.*

lies in a system of resource use whose "hallmark is the use of state power to systematically undervalue biomass . . . and organize its supply to those in power at highly subsidized values." Gadgil sites the famous case of Karnataka's bamboo. Before 1960, the Forest Department supplied bamboo to local basket-weavers and the crop had a commercial value of around 3,000 rupees a tonne. However, once West Coast Paper Mills was set up in Uttar Kannada district, the Forest Department began to supply the mills with bamboo – an ideal raw material for paper manufacture – at a nominal cost of one rupee a tonne. Before long Karnataka's bamboo had been virtually wiped out, and the mills cast their rapacious net first to neighbouring Andhra Pradesh, then to the Garhwal Himalaya and finally to Assam and Nagaland. By grossly undervaluing a natural resource, the authorities have encouraged its destruction; the environment has suffered, local villagers have

suffered, and so have Karnataka's basket-weavers. "The undervaluing of biomass to ensure its subsidized supply to the commercial sector", concluded Gadgil, "has been achieved by abolishing the traditional rights of rural society." In fact, everything that has happened in the sphere of forest use over the past two centuries has worked against those for whom, in Mr Rawal's words, forests act as a life-support system. Deprived of their traditional rights to harvest the produce of the forests, many have come to view them as symbols of an authority they despise. Instead of protecting the forests, as their forebears had, they abuse them: the principal victims of deforestation have now become a major cause of it.

Conservation is often said to be a luxury which only the rich can afford; however, many of India's rural poor are beginning to realize that conservation is a necessity, and in every part of the country villagers are coming together to save their forests from further abuse. They are the heirs to an honourable tradition of non-violent resistance, first seen in India's forests over three centuries ago. In 1610, two Bishnoi women were killed while trying to prevent the felling of a khejri tree in the village of Ramasari, near Jodhpur in Rajasthan. Forty-three years later, seventeen Bishnois were killed for the same reason, but this was a minor incident compared to one which took place several generations later. In 1730 the ruler of Jodhpur ordered the felling of more khejri trees to provide construction timber for his palace. A total of 363 Bishnois were killed while trying to protect them. Survivors counted their dead, cremated them, then walked to Jodhpur to complain to the maharajah. Shocked by the havoc wreaked by his axemen, the maharajah issued a decree that henceforth no green tree could ever be cut in a Bishnoi village.

A gathering of Bishnoi women: their ancestors gave their lives to
save the forests near Jodhpur.

Throughout the British era, colonial forestry practices sparked off sporadic protests, which generally took the form of *satyagrahas*, or non-violent resistance. *Satyagrahas* greeted the Forest Acts of 1878 and 1927, both of which furthered the commercial aspirations of the British while restricting the villagers' right to use their forests. The authorities reacted harshly to these protests, murdering Gond tribals in central India, and killing dozens of villagers in the Garhwal Himalaya. Fittingly, the Garhwal later gave birth to a movement which achieved world-wide fame. In December 1972 the villagers of Purola, Uttarkashi and Gopeshwar held a series of meetings to protest against the commercial exploitation of their forests. One of the leading activists was the folk-poet Ghanshyam Raturi, whose poem describing the method by which the forests were to be saved gave the movement its name:

> Embrace the trees
> Save them from being felled;
> The property of our hills,
> Save them from being looted.

The word in Hindi for embrace is *"chipko"*, and this was the beginning of a movement which was to spread rapidly across these Himalayan foothills. In April 1973 a sports manufacturer from Allahabad sent a team of contractors to a village near Gopeshwar to cut down ten ash trees. The villagers protected the trees by embracing them and eventually the axemen left. Scenes such as this, often involving much greater numbers, became commonplace throughout this part of the Himalaya, with the women at the forefront of Chipko activities. The state forest department was forced to rethink its policies, and following a meeting with Sunderlal Bahuguna, Mrs

Gandhi recommended that there should be a fifteen-year ban on commercial green felling in Uttar Pradesh's Himalayan forests. Chipko's demand that the Himalayan forests should be declared "protection forests" was also met.

This moratorium gave Bahuguna time to spread the Chipko message to other parts of India. In 1981 he marched over 3,000 miles along the Himalaya, from Kashmir in the west to Kohima in the east, to campaign against deforestation and alert the villagers to the philosophy and achievements of the Chipko movement. This was the first of many long walks, and his proselytizing has been enormously influential. For example, in 1983 Bahuguna visited Karnataka's Uttar Kannada district, an area ravaged by deforestation, and inspired villagers to launch a tree-embracing movement. It became known as *"Appiko"*, which means Chipko in the local Kannada language. The Appiko movement has achieved much in its short life, and its activists have carried their message along the length of the Western Ghats and far beyond.

Chipko and Appiko began by being obstructive, but both have successfully promoted a range of activities to enhance the environment and improve the fortunes of the villagers. While Bahuguna was tramping the countryside, the Chipko villagers set about afforesting their scarred hills. With the help of university students, workers with voluntary agencies and others, the Chipko women have re-planted thousands of acres of land around their villages. They have also introduced measures to protect the forests from overgrazing by domestic livestock and they have set up gobar-gas plants to reduce the consumption of fuelwood. Meanwhile, in the hills of Kamataka, the Appiko movement is following Chipko's example and is pursuing its own eco-development programmes.

*Double vision: while Nehru saw big dams and grandiose
development projects as "the temples of the future", Mahatma
Gandhi yearned for a more ascetic, village-based way of
life. India's modern leaders are not always sure
what they want.*

Overwhelmed by the sheer magnitude of the country's problems, there are some people in India who hold out little hope for the future. They believe that for the vast majority of her inhabitants, whose lives are already tainted by poverty, things can only get worse, and they foresee the day when much of the countryside will be so disfigured by deforestation, erosion and other environmental ills that it will sustain neither humans nor wildlife. These harbingers of doom are expressing legitimate fears which spring from the misery and desolation they observe around them; but while they choose to await the apocalypse, tens of thousands, indeed millions of others are doing their best to ensure it never comes.

A recent survey carried out by the World Wide Fund for Nature suggests that there are now over 900 environmental groups in India. They vary enormously, both in terms of size and aspirations.

Excavations for the Kaiga nuclear power station, Karnataka. Environmentalists in India have been bitterly opposed to the nuclear programme.

Some, like Chipko and Appiko, have concentrated on saving existing forests and establishing new ones. Others, like the now celebrated village of Ralegun Siddhi in Maharashtra, have tackled everything from alcoholism to health care, from animal husbandry to forestry. Indeed, the 'greening' of India's villages may be looked upon as one of the great achievements of the 1980s and 1990s. Across the country, villagers are working out their own solutions to problems which higher authorities have ignored – and sometimes caused; pockets of poverty are gradually becoming paradigms of plenty.

Nowhere in India has the power of the meek to change the course of history been more brilliantly demonstrated than in Kusnur, a picturesque, thatch-roofed village of some 6,000 people nestling in the dry, red-earth foothills of the Western Ghats. I arrived here one sweltering pre-monsoon morning with Chikkappa, a young man born in a neighbouring village and now a project officer with the India Development Service (IDS), a voluntary organisation established in 1979 to promote rural development. Within a few minutes Chikkappa had gathered together a farmer, a miller and a goldsmith; the morning began to take on a Chaucerian feel. We sat in the mill and the three villagers recounted the background to their struggle against Karnataka Pulpwood Ltd (KPL), a joint sector company established in 1984 with 51 per cent of its shares owned by the Karnataka government and the rest by Harihar Polyfibres, a vast industrial concern which turns wood into viscose. 30,000 hectares of land had been given to KPL by the government in order for it to grow eucalyptus to supply Harihar Polyfibres with the raw materials to fuel its lucrative operations. The company became very active in the hills around Kusnur and before long 400 hectares of forested land

B. J. Jujaghau, a goldsmith and 'pluck and plant' activist
in Kusnur, discussing the future of a failed eucalyptus plantation
with Chikkappa, a project officer with the India
Development Service.

fruit and timber; bamboo for basket-making; others for green manure, gum and leaves with which to make the traditional plates used at weddings and festivals. They watered and tended these saplings but after a while the KPL guards destroyed most of them. The following year the exercise was repeated; this time 52 villagers, including those who recounted the story now, were arrested by the police.

We finished our tea and headed for the plantation. Had I come a year ago I would have seen the hillsides covered with 20-foot-high eucalyptus trees, but villagers had taken matters into their own hands and in less than four weeks the entire 400-hectare plantation had been stripped of its trees. "We didn't support that action," explained Sammadasab Mulla, the miller, "but it showed how angry people had become around here." The eucalyptus stumps were beginning to sprout again and there remained still a few of the more useful trees which the pluck and plant activists had introduced.

While the people of Kusnur cast themselves in the role of David against the Goliath of Karnataka Pulpwood Ltd – and pitted themselves against both the state government and the immensely influential Birla family, the owners of Harihar Polyfibres – Samaj Parivartana Samudaya filed a public interest suit against KPL and others in the Supreme Court, obtaining a stay order preventing further planting by the company in May 1987. The state government subsequently transferred a further 30,000 acres of land to KPL. S. R. Hiremath, SPS's charismatic leader, immediately filed a contempt of court petition. His organisation also briefed the banks which were backing the project about the illegalities of the 'land grab' and many others joined the campaign against KPL. In the end the pressure proved irresistible and on 3 October 1991 the Karnataka cabinet decided to

beside the village had been taken over, bulldozed, and planted with eucalyptus saplings. "At one time" recalled B. S. Jujaghau, the goldsmith, "these hills were covered with good forest. When I was a child we used to get all sorts of animals here – tiger, blackbuck, wild pig, peacock. Now there's nothing: all the wildlife has been driven away . . ."

Not long after KPL had destroyed the old forest and replaced it with eucalyptus, a useless tree as far as villagers are concerned, an environmental pressure group called Samaj Parivartana Samudaya (SPS), a sister organisation of the IDS and exponent of non-violent direct action, held some workshops in Kusnur. "We decided we had to act," recalled Ningappa Baligar, the farmer, "and in 1987 we came up with the idea of a Kittiko-Hachchiko *satyagraha*". Loosely translated, this means "pluck and plant", which is precisely what the villagers did. They marched on the KPL plantation, plucked out 100 eucalyptus saplings and planted in their place trees which they considered useful: tamarind for its fodder, fruit and firewood; mango and jackfruit for

The landless women of Holtikoti village in Karnataka
supplement their earnings by making plates from the leaves of
the muttala *tree.*

*Amanullakhan Soudagar, a farmer in Aironi village, says he
will continue to fight against the companies polluting the
Tungabhadra River.*

throw in the towel: KPL, it was announced, was to be wound up.

"We are very happy that the project has been cancelled," explained Ningappa as we made our way through the stunted remains of the eucalyptus plantation, "but the struggle is not over yet. Now we've got to make sure that this land is used for the benefit of all the villagers. What we want to do is plant it with the sorts of trees which we need." A few miles away from Kusnur, the villagers of Kerekaytanhalli had already dug 3,500 pits in an 80-acre patch of eucalyptus recently abandoned by the KPL forest guards. Soon the monsoons would arrive and the pits would become home to mango, neem, tamarind, bamboo and many other species essential to the survival of an Indian village.

I left Kusnur and the surrounding villages in high spirits; here, it seemed, were men and women with the strength to fight against predatory industrial concerns and the wit to turn barren lands into fields of plenty. But my joy was short-lived, for the sword which Harihar Polyfibres wields against the environment is double-edged and exceedingly sharp. On the one hand, its appetite for eucalyptus has led to the destruction of much native forest and the appropriation of land previously used by villagers, either to graze their stock, or to satisfy their needs for fuelwood, fruits and so forth. On the other, the waste products generated by the factories at Harihar have led to the chronic pollution of the Tungabhadra River. There was nothing to lift the spirits in the village of Aironi, which sat by the wide river in the lee of a ruined fort some ten miles downstream from the factories. "Ever since the factory started up in 1972 our lives have been blighted by pollution," said Amanullakhan Soudagar, a young farmer who accompanied us to the water's edge. There were 50 or so people washing themselves and their clothes in the river – "but none of them are from Aironi," explained Amanullakhan. Apparently, they had come for a festival the day before and they would be heading homewards shortly. Local *dhobis* had given up using the water here to wash their laundry as the pollution rotted the clothes.

Amanullakhan farmed 23 acres of riverside land; heavy-metal pollution of the water which irrigated his fields had led to a serious decline in crop yields and a drop in the oil content of his paddy. He had been involved in numerous non-violent protests against the factories at Harihar and pressure from the villagers, combined with widespread agitation spearheaded by SPS, had led to some marginal improvements in water quality. "We'll continue to protest until the factories stop polluting our river," vowed Amanullakhan when we left him.

The people who have suffered most have been the fishermen along the Tungabhadra, the vast majority of whom are landless and have no other means of making a living. A miserable group gathered to meet us in the village: many were painfully thin and, I suspect, hungry. Fakeerappa Pyatimoni said that before the factories were built they used to be able to catch between 10 and 15 kilos of fish in a day; now they were lucky if they got one kilo. The pollution rotted their nets, he explained, and gave them such severe skin problems that few risked going in the river more than once a day at a time. At the mention of this, two elderly fishermen came forward, raised their *lungis* and showed me their legs, which were covered with weeping sores. "We'll carry on fighting till our river is clean again" said Fakeerappa, though he and all the others I spoke to there well aware of the political clout of their foe. Fortunately, these fishermen have Samaj Parivartana Samudaya on their side: as the Karnatakaa government and the Birlas discovered during the KPL struggle, SPS is a formidable opponent.

Many of the 900-odd groups listed in the WWF's survey adopt a multi-disciplinary approach to the environment. SPS is a good example of an organisation which fights on many fronts. Since it was founded by S. R. Hiremath in 1984, it has campaigned against the industrial pollution of the Tungabhadra River; it has fought alongside villagers and tribals to save native forests from destruction, it has helped to influence for the better a large social forestry project funded by the World Bank and the British Government; and it played a prominent role in organizing the Save the Western Ghats March. While SPS adopts a confrontational approach to tackling the environmental problems in Karnataka, its sister organization, the India Development Service concentrates on the nitty-gritty of helping villagers to raise their standards of living and restore their degraded surroundings.

Another organization which has taken a broad approach is the Kerala Sastra Sahitya Parishad. KSSP began by fighting poverty and social injustice, and by promoting small-scale development projects and better health care. Its interest in matters environmental date from the early 1970s when it helped to investigate the pollution around the port of Cochin; it became a household name in India later in the decade when it successfully spearheaded the campaign to save Silent Valley from a hydro-electric power project. In 1988 KSSP was awarded the Indira Gandhi Paryavaran Puraskar. The organization, read the citation, "has rendered significant service to the cause of environmental protection through scientific analysis of environmental issues and through spreading awareness of these issues among the masses."

Ignorance destroys; knowledge saves. That is why nearly every environmental organization operating in India today lays great store in education. With so

A world of contrasts: country dwellers bring their skills to a city fair in Bombay.

many groups and individuals active in this field, it seems invidious to single out one or two while ignoring the rest. However, I shall throw propriety to the winds and mention two organizations, one in Bombay, the other in Calcutta, which in their very different ways are seeking to improve the quality of life for city-dwellers and spread the conservation message through every sector of the population.

If you find yourself in Bombay with half a day to spare I suggest that you catch a train from Victoria Terminus, the finest example of tropical Gothic architecture in the world, descend at Sion station and take the No. 165 bus to the Dharavi Bus Depot. On your way there you will pass beside the Dharavi slums, which constitute one of India's grimmer urban landscapes. Had you come here five or six years ago you would have been treated to the most unedifying sight: opposite the depot there used to be a mountain of domestic garbage, laced with decaying animal carcasses and virtually every other type of waste imaginable. Rubbish in India always has a value and over twenty different sorts of organized picker used to work this tip: some specialized in rags, others in rubber or plastic or copper wire; several even made a living retrieving gold rings which had been carelessly jettisoned with the household refuse. The rubbish tip has gone and today's visitor, on crossing the road outside the bus depot, walks into a beautiful, densely wooded park.

I came to Mahim Nature Park, as it is now known, in the company of the Project Coordinator, an articulate, witty, vivacious woman called Shanta Chatterji. At one time, she explained, there were plans to develop Mahim Creek for industry, but fortunately the local authority decided to invite the public to participate in determining its future. Shanta was a prominent figure within the World Wide Fund

for Nature – first as secretary of the Western Region and later as chairwoman for Maharashtra and Goa – and she and her colleagues realized that the site had tremendous potential for environmental education. They put forward a proposal for a nature park and the Bombay Metropolitan Region Development Authority decided to back them. Since 1983 the BMRDA has funded the development of the park, which consists of thirty-seven acres of reclaimed land and 450 acres of mangrove swamp and marsh.

One of the great things about a humid tropical climate is that vegetation grows with astonishing rapidity. (On the day of our visit it was 82 °F, which prompted a headline in the local paper which read "Cold Snap to Continue".) Many of the 12,000 trees and shrubs planted since 1983 are now well beyond their adolescence and it is hard to believe that this was a rubbish tip less than a decade ago. "When we first started work, this whole area was used as a latrine," explained Shanta as we wandered into the medicinal plants garden. "We fenced off one section, and as we planted trees and cut the grass, people receded! Once the slum-dwellers realized that the park would improve their environment, they were very co-operative."

We spent an hour or so wandering along the park's nature trails – there was an eco trail, a renewable energy trail, a web-of-life trail, a medicinal plants trail and a marine trail – and eventually arrived at the Environmental Education Centre, a circular building recently completed and awaiting its first batch of visitors. We sat in the shade with Shanta's husband – together they run a company which manufactures electric cars – and ate a picnic of chapatis, dahl and lemongrass tea. "In India," said Shanta, "people tend to think of 'environment' as a Western concept. We've got to get round this and the way we're doing

it is through our culture and mythology. Every villager is familiar with the Hindu myths and epics and we emphasize the fact that Indians have traditionally been great conservationists." After lunch we wandered round the astral garden: "Each birth sign is associated with one or more trees," explained Shanta, "and if you meditate under your particular tree, it's supposed to bring you health and prosperity." She stationed me beneath a clump of bamboo, the tree associated with Cancerians: "To be Indian is to be aware of trees and a lover of trees," she said bluntly. There were twenty-seven different species of tree around us, each with a stone on which were painted the astral sign and the name of the tree in both Hindu and English. "When people come here", said Shanta, "we'll show them these five trees" – she pointed to a pipal, an umber, a palas, a mango and a banyan – "and we'll tell them that Indians have been planting these trees in sacred groves and beside temples for thousands of years. In fact, planting trees is one thing that everyone can do."

Although the casual visitor can turn up at any time to wander through the astral garden, follow a nature trail or watch the flocks of egrets and waders feeding in the marshland, the majority of visitors – the Mahim Nature Trust expects a third of a million a year – will come in organized parties. "Many groups which play an important role in society need to be educated about the way their activities affect the environment," explained Shanta. "So we're not just targeting schoolchildren and students, although they're important. We'll be taking groups from the police, from hotels, from the railways, from industry. We've also got to get the decision-makers." The centre is staffed by experts in the field of environmental education, and within a few years the trust hopes that its library will house 10,000 books.

Environmental education should be enlightening; it should also be fun, and Shanta talked of their plans to use theatre, film, dance, art and other media to get the message across in an entertaining way. "We want people to think about the consequences of their actions," said Shanta, and indeed that is one of the prime objectives of every environmental education project in India, whether it is aimed at helping village women learn about the efficient use of fuel, teaching railway staff about waste (polystyrene cups have recently taken over from recyclable clay cups), or encouraging urban children to appreciate the countryside. The Mahim Nature Park has been imaginatively conceived and wonderfully executed, and it is just one of the many thousands of projects which foster a better understanding of the natural world in India.

"If I die now," Baba Amte once said, "I would like them to put on my grave a line like the one on crossed cheques – 'a man who said responsibility is not transferable'." The greatest challenge for those involved in India's environmental movement lies in convincing people that they are capable of changing the world for the better, and that responsibility, as Baba Amte put it, is not transferable. In cities like Calcutta, apathy is as tangible as the reek of poverty. "Find, if you can, a more uninviting stop than Calcutta," wrote Sir George Trevelyan in 1863. "It unites every condition of a perfectly unhealthy situation . . . the place is so bad by nature that human effort could do little to make it worse; but that little has been done faithfully and assiduously." Well, the Calcutta of today is no better, indeed probably far worse a place to live in than it was in Trevelyan's day, when its population was less than a million, its slums minute compared to those you will see now. "The problems here are so immense", explained

Pradeep Kakkar, "that many people have just given up." I met Pradeep, his wife Bonari and two other founders of PUBLIC, People United for Better Living in Calcutta, after they had finished work one evening. "We believe that if there's to be an improvement in the city's living conditions," said Pradeep, "or if we are ever going to arrest the decline, we can't leave things for agencies appointed by government. They've proved themselves in-capable; there's much too much apathy there." So far PUBLIC has concentrated on issues to do with Calcutta's environment and citizens' rights. "We're trying to promote the idea that everyone should feel a responsibility for the way things are," said Bonari. "We have a right to a decent environment – to clean air and clean water – and we are forcing the authorities to realize that."

During its short life, PUBLIC has mounted several successful campaigns. It began by organizing "A March for Power" to protest against the city's dreadful record of electricity supply. "WE ARE FED UP," declaimed the march poster. "We don't want to know about wet coal and about sabotage and pilferage . . . we simply want that minimal level of electricity in our homes and offices and classrooms and hospitals that people all over India are getting. And we want a PERMANENT IMPROVEMENT, not only for the Pujas or the World Cup!" This campaign has embarrassed the authorities into improving power supply. PUBLIC asked that in-efficient state-run plants should be handed over to the private sector, and so far one plant has been. Calcutta's citizens are now given, for the first time, advance notification of power cuts. PUBLIC has also mounted a campaign to reduce noise levels near schools and hospitals, and Calcutta's police cooperate in enforcing the "NO HORN – SILENCE ZONES".

Among other things, PUBLIC is raising awareness about pollution in the Hooghly River and the shortcomings of the Ganga Action Plan, and it has been a key player in the battle to save the East Calcutta Marshes from the profiteers who wish to turn the fish ponds and vegetable farms into housing for the rich.

Nowadays so much media attention is focused on the exploits of Gandhian activists like Sunderlal Bahuguna and Baba Amte, and on village organiza-tions like Chipko and Appiko, that one could be forgiven for thinking that India's environmental movement was a sort of peasant uprising. And to some extent it is, but one of the great strengths of the environmental movement is its diversity. The small band of people who run PUBLIC belong to the professional classes. "We don't have to apologize for not being members of the down-trodden," said Pradeep. "The Communist government here has always painted things along class lines, but class is irrelevant to what we're doing. What matters is that people have the ideological strength to speak out for what they believe." And people from every sector of society, from every class, religion and race, are beginning to speak out.

My travels in India ended where they began, on the coast of Gujarat. Captain Adam's trawler deposited me in Salaya one warm, breezy mid-morning, and a couple of hours later I arrived at Jamnagar's splendidly shabby Hotel Aram. I had scarcely had time to wash, eat and have a cut-throat shave at a nearby barber's, when two young men with a story to tell arrived at the hotel. Himanshu Prem and Nigam Pandya were two thirds of the way through a 1000-kilometre walk whose purpose was to focus public attention on the Asiatic lion, to raise funds for Gir national park and to spread the

Winnowing rice. Sorting the grain from the chaff – the good development projects from the bad – must be the principal aim of tomorrow's politicians if rural India, her people and her wildlife are to survive.

conservation message in the Gujarat countryside. Himanshu and Nigam had been on the road for over a month, yet they seemed remarkably fresh and they were looking ahead to the next 300 kilometres and two weeks with unbridled enthusiasm. We decided to find somewhere peaceful to talk, climbed into an autorickshaw and headed for Lakota Lake, a large tank not far from the centre of town with two balustraded causeways leading to an old palace. The causeways were lined with cormorants, pigeons and gulls and on a sandbank in one corner there were half a dozen painted storks, four demoiselle cranes, a pond heron and some sleeping ducks. Three pelicans moved swiftly through the water like galleons off to war and two kingfishers fished energetically in the shade of a pipal tree.

We sat down on a flight of steps near the palace. "We're trying to educate the youngsters about the problem which the Asiatic lion faces," began Himanshu. "Most people in Gujarat don't even realize that there's just one population of lions left." So far they'd talked to over 6,000 children, not only about the lion but about Gujarat's other endangered wildlife. Himanshu produced a roughly manufactured bullet from his overalls. "We found this near the blackbuck sanctuary at Velavadar," he explained, "so it seems that they are still being poached"; blackbuck, chinkara, sloth bear and tiger all faced an uncertain future in Gujarat. I asked whether the villagers thought this "Walk for Vanraj" – walk for the king of the forest – eccentric. "No, I don't think so," replied Nigam. All the same, these slightly built characters with their dungarees spattered with badges must have presented a curious spectacle. They carried a mascot of a lion wherever they went and this had a pied-piper effect on the children they encountered. "Sometimes, soon after we've entered a remote village", explained Himanshu, "we turn round to find that we have 200 or 300 children following us. They always want to touch the lion and to know what we're doing."

The walk was taking Himanshu and Nigam through twelve sanctuaries and national parks in Gujarat. "It's not a protest march," said Nigam. "Many people in the Forest Department want to do their bit for conservation, but they need public support and that's where we can help. We can bridge the gap between the people and the government." Did they, I enquired, really think this walk would have some influence. "Yes," said Himanshu without hesitation. "We've come across so many young people who are keen to do something for conservation. At the moment they aren't part of any established network. Now, if we could get them to work for conservation in the remote parts of Gujarat, that would *really* be something."

Before we parted company we stopped at the edge of the lake to watch a third kingfisher, this one the small russet-and-azure variety familiar to fishermen in Europe, bashing the head of a silver fish against a branch. A querulous flock of rose-ringed parakeets dashed above our heads and on the far side of the lake the painted storks rose from the sandbank and flew with marvellous grace across the city's roofs. The kingfisher gulped down his meal, and Himanshu and Nigam set off once again on their long walk. Over the past few months I had seen many things in India which filled me with gloom, but there were times when I was overwhelmed by the sheer splendour of the place, by the beauty and generosity of its inhabitants, and by the courage and dedication of people like Himanshu and Nigam – two foot-soldiers in the ever-growing army of people who were determined to make India a better place to live in.

Acknowledgements

◆

I owe a great debt of gratitude to the following people, some of whom I have written about and all of whom helped, advised and entertained me during my travels around their remarkable country: Shankho Chowdhury, Amit Roy, Pradeep Kakkar and Bonari Kakkar of People United for Better Living in Calcutta; Eddie and Cecilia d'Souza; Ranjan Kamath of RKO Films, Calcutta; Dr Dhrubajyoti Ghosh; Devika Sircar of the World Wide Fund for Nature (WWF), Calcutta; Dr R. B. Grubh and S. A. Hussein of the Bombay Natural History Society; Shanta Chatterji and Dhiren Panya at Mahim Nature Park, Bombay; Dr J. C. Punetha of WWF, Bombay; Baba Amte, Kisan Mehta, Ramesh Kacholia, Arvind Adarkar, Pankaj Mantri, Vibhash Sureka, Om Prakesh Rawal and many others involved in the Narmada struggle; Dr Seshagiri Rao and Mrs Padma Srinivasan of the Family Planning Association of India; Pradeep Pandya and Narendrasinh Jhala of WWF, Rajkot; the late Professor R. M. Naik and Dr Rishad Pravez of Saurashtra University; Dr Smita Krishnan; Shyamal Tikader of Gir lion sanctuary; N. D. Jayal of the Indian National Trust for Art and Cultural Heritage; Thomas Mathew, Sharad Gaur and P. Chatterjee of WWF, New Delhi; R. L. Singh, formerly of Project Tiger; Rajiv Jain of CENDIT; Toby Sinclair; A. Bhattacharya; D. N. Mazumda; Dr A. J. T. Johnsingh of the Wildlife Institute of India; Ravi Chellam; Preston Ahimaz of WWF, Madras; Shekkar Dattatri and Revati Muckerjee of Ecomedia, Madras; Harry Andrews of the Madras Crocodile Bank; Dipankar Ghosh; Shebbar Sheerazi; John Fernandez of

the Programme for Community Organisation, Trivandrum; Brian O'Riordan of the Intermediate Technology Development Group; Steve Creech; V. Vivekanandan; Aleyamma Vijayan; N. Mohanraj, Matheen Sait and Mr R. Radcliffe of the Nilgiri Wildlife and Environment Association; Roland Martins of Jagrut Goenkaranchi Fouz (JGF), Goa; Claude Alvares of the Goa Founda-

tion; S. R. and Shyamala Hiremath of the Samaj Parivartana Samudaya (SPS) and India Development Service (IDS), Karnataka; G. K. Chikkappa, R. B. Patil, P. V. Patil and T. S. Pathan of IDS, Medleri; Dr R. R. Kongovi, Dharwad; Ningappa F. Baligar, Sammadasab Mulla and B. S. Jujaghau of Kusnur village, Dharwad district; and the farmers and fishermen of Aironi village, on the banks of the polluted Tungabhadra River.

There are several other people who deserve a special word of thanks. Gillian Wright, who acted as a fixer for the *Wild India* series, went to extraordinary lengths to make my journeys around India, and those of the television crews, infinitely easier and more pleasurable than they would otherwise have been. While Gillian orchestrated our movements from New Delhi, Veronique Seifert of North-South Productions was responsible for looking after matters in London. She handled this difficult task with great charm and remarkable patience. *In Search of Wild India* features the work of some outstanding photographers; my thanks in particular go to Michael Pitts, a television cameraman based in Hong Kong, Sunjoy Monga of Bombay and Roderick Johnson of "Images of India". Between them they have provided the bulk of the photographs. Responsibility for finding and choosing the photographs has rested with Shana Magraw, who has been a delight to work with. My final thanks go to Richard Keefe of North-South Productions. He conceived the idea for the television series *Wild India*, and brought it to fruition. Without his energy and inspiration neither the series nor this book would have seen the light of day.

Selected Bibliography

◆

Agarwal, A. et al., *The Second Citizen's Report on the Environment 1987*, New Delhi, Centre for Science and Environment, 1987.

Agarwal, A. et al., *The State of India's Environment 1982*, New Delhi, Centre for Science and Environment, 1982.

Agarwal, A. & Narain, S., *Towards Green Villages*, New Delhi, Centre for Science and Environment, 1989.

Ali, Salim, *The Book of Indian Birds* Bombay, Natural History Society, 1941.

Alvares, Claude, and Billorey, Ramesh, *Damming the Narmada*, Penang, Third World Network, 1988.

Bandyopadhyay, J. et al. (eds), *India's Environment – Crises and Responses*, Dehra Dun, Natraj, 1985.

Bedi, Rajesh and Ramesh, *Indian Wildlife*, New Delhi, 1984.

Burton, R. G., *Sport and Wildlife in the Deccan*, London, Hutchinson, 1928.

Cleves Moss, Julia, *India – Paths to Development*, Oxford, Oxfam, 1991.

Corbett, Jim, *Man-Eaters of Kumaon*, Bombay, Oxford University Press, 1944.

Corbett, Jim, *The Temple Tiger*, Bombay, Oxford University Press, 1954.

Craven, Roy C., *Indian Art*, London, Thames & Hudson, 1976.

Daniel, J. C. (ed.), *A Century of Natural History*, Bombay, Bombay Natural History Society, 1983.

Davies, Philip, *The Penguin Guide to the Monuments of India, Volume II: Islamic, Rajput, European*, London, Penguin, 1989.

D'Monte, Darryl, *Temples or Tombs? Industry versus Environment: Three Controversies*, New Delhi, Centre for Science and Environment, 1985.

Hawkins, R. E., *Encyclopedia of Indian Natural History*, New Delhi, Oxford University Press, 1986.

Israel, Samuel, and Sinclair, Toby (eds), *Indian Wildlife*, Singapore, Apa Productions, 1988.

Michell, George, *The Penguin Guide to the Monuments of India, Volume I: Buddhist, Jain, Hindu*, London, Penguin, 1989.

Moorhouse, Geoffrey, *Calcutta – The City Revealed*, London, Penguin, 1974.

Mountford, Guy, *Saving the Tiger*, London, Michael Joseph, 1981.

Paranjpye, Vijay, *High Dams on the Narmada*, New Delhi, INTACH, 1990.

Polo, Marco, *The Travels*, London, Penguin, 1958.

Ravi, N. (ed), *The Hindu Survey of Indian Agriculture 1991*, Madras, Rangarajan, 1991.

Ravi, N. (ed), *The Hindu Survey of the Environment 1991*, Madras, Rangarajan, 1991.

Saxena, Ghanshyam, *The Forest Crisis*, Dehra Dun, Natraj, 1990.

Spear, P., *A History of India, Volume 2: From the Sixteenth Century to the Twentieth Century*, London, Penguin, 1978.

Thapar, R., *A History of India, Volume 1: From the Discovery of India to 1526*, London, Penguin, 1966.

Watson, Francis, *A Concise History of India*, London, Thames & Hudson, 1974.

Woodcock, Martin, *Collins Handguide to the Birds of the Indian Sub-Continent*, London, Collins, 1980.

von Furer-Haimendorf, Christoph, *Tribes of India – The Struggle for Survival*, New Delhi, Oxford University Press, 1985.

The books listed above are but a small fraction of the vast body of literature which deals with the Indian environment. I have found all of these in some way illuminating or useful, but I have also relied on several other sources:

The admirable *Sanctuary* magazine provides good bi-monthly coverage of India's environmental issues (all queries to Sanctuary Asia, No. 602 Maker Chamber V, Nariman Point, Bombay 400 021).

The Bombay Natural History Society publishes a learned journal and *Hornbill*, a somewhat lighter newsletter to members (all queries to BNHS, Hornbill House, Shahid Bhagat Singh road, Bombay 400 023). BNHS has published many books and pamphlets on wildlife and conservation issues.

The Indian Natural Trust for Art and Cultural Heritage (INTACH) has published over a dozen booklets in its excellent environmental series. It has also published major studies of the environmental impact of the Narmada and Tehri dams. INTACH's head office is at 71, Lodi Estate, New Delhi 110 003.

The World Wide Fund for Nature (WWF) has also produced some excellent material. Its Environmental Services Group has published a long list of titles under the unprepossessing heading of "Documentation of the Experience in Environmental Management". These include studies of the Bombay Environmental Action Group, the Appiko movement, the Madras Crocodile Bank, the Doon Valley, Silent Valley and many other organisations and topics mentioned in this book. WWF has offices throughout India; its headquarters are at 172B, Lodi Estate, New Delhi 110 003.

Index

Photographic Credits

◆

Cover R. C. Nutbrown/Images of India
Back cover Vivek R. Sinha/Survival Anglia
Page 1 Sunjoy Monga/Porpoise
     Photostock
2 A. Acharya/Images of India
3 Roderick Johnson/Images of India
5 Roderick Johnson/Images of India
6 Michael Pitts
9 M. A. Malini/DPA/Images of India
10 Sunjoy Monga/Porpoise Photostock
11 Roderick Johnson/Images of India
12 Roderick Johnson/Images of India
12 J. Alex Langley/Aspect Picture
     Library
14 Sunjoy Monga/Porpoise Photostock
16 Vivek Singha/Survival Anglia
18 British Library
19 Sunjoy Monga/Porpoise Photostock
20 Sunjoy Monga/Porpoise Photostock
22 Charlie Pye-Smith
23 David R. Austen/Bruce Coleman
24 Jeff Foott/Survival Anglia
25 Michael Pitts
26 Peter Menzel/Impact
27 Roderick Johnson/Images of India
28 D. Banerjee/DPA/Images of India
29 Roderick Johnson/Images of India
31 Suraj N. Sharma/Images of India
32 Douglas Dickins F.R.P.S.
34 Roderick Johnson/Images of India
35 Sunjoy Monga/Porpoise Photostock
36 N. M. Kelvalkar/Images of India
37 Charlie Pye Smith
38 Hutchinson Library
39 Tim Beddow/Hutchinson Library
42 Hutchinson Library
42 Tim Beddow/Hutchinson Library
45 N. Madhwani/DPA/Images of India
46 Christine Pemberton/Hutchinson
     Library
47 Michael Pitts
49 Douglas Dickins F.R.P.S.
50 Charlie Pye-Smith
51 Roderick Johnson/Images of India

52 Toby Sinclair
54 Roderick Johnson/Images of India
55 Michael Pitts
56 Anil A. Dave/DPA/Images of India
58 S. Nagaraj/DPA/Images of India
60 S. Nagaraj/DPA/Images of India
61 Sunjoy Monga/Porpoise Photostock
62 Roderick Johnson/Images of India
64 Firoze Mistry/Images of India
65 Sunjoy Monga/Porpoise Photostock
66 Sunjoy Monga/Porpoise Photostock
68 Images of India
69 R. A.Acharya/DPA/Images of India
71 Sunjoy Monga/Porpoise Photostock
72 Charlie Pye-Smith
73 Sunjoy Monga/Porpoise Photostock
74 Sunjoy Monga/Porpoise Photostock
76 Helene Rogers/Trip
78 Sunjoy Monga/Porpoise Photostock
79 Sunjoy Monga/Porpoise Photostock
80 Hutchinson Library
83 M & V Birley/Trepix
84 Roderick Johnson/Images of India
85 Roderick Johnson/Images of India
89 R. Bhaliat/DPA/Images of India
90 Helene Rogers/Trip
92 Helene Rogers/Trip
94 S. Nagaraj/DPA/Images of India
98 Roderick Johnson/Images of India
98 Images of India
98 Images of India
100 Roderick Johnson/Images of India
101 Sunjoy Monga/Porpoise Photostock
103 P. Bokarifi/Images of India
104 Roderick Johnson/Images of India
106 V. I. Thayil/DPA/Images of India
109 British Library
110 Sunjoy Monga/Porpose Photostock
112 J. Mehta/DPA/Images of India
115 Dave Brintcombe/Hutchinson
     Library
116 S. Nagaraj/DPA/Images of India
117 S. Nagaraj/DPA/Images of India
119 Sunjoy Monga/Porpoise Photostock

120 Roderick Johnson/Images of India
121 Roderick Johnson/Images of India
121 Roderick Johnson/Images of India
122 R. A. Acharya/DPA/Images of India
124 Prashant Bokaria/Images of India
129 Roderick Johnson/Images of India
130 Roderick Johnson/Images of India
132 Alex Langley/Aspect Picture Library
134 Charlie Pye-Smith
135 Charlie Pye-Smith
137 R. A. Acharya/DPA/Images of India
138 Michael Pitts
139 Michael Pitts
139 Michael Pitts
140 Michael Pitts
143 Michael Pitts
144 Michael Pitts
146 Michael Pitts
148 Roderick Johnson/Images of India
149 Roderick Johnson/Images of India
150 Charlie Pye-Smith
152 Sunjoy Monga/Porpoise Photostock
153 Sunjoy Monga/Porpoise Photostock
154 Sunjoy Monga/Porpoise Photostock
156 Roderick Johnson/Images of India
156 Roderick Johnson/Images of India
159 Sunjoy Monga/Porpoise Photostock
160 Sunjoy Monga/Porpoise Photostock
162 Roderick Johnson/Images of India
164 Charlie Pye-Smith
166 Roderick Johnson/Images of India
168 Roderick Johnson/Images of India
171 Hutchinson Library
172 Roderick Johnson/Images of India
173 Sunjoy Monga/Porpoise Photostock
175 M. Parpiani/DPA/Images of India
176 Images of India
178 Charlie Pye-Smith
179 Charlie Pye-Smith
180 Charlie Pye-Smith
183 Sunjoy Monga/Porpoise Photostock
187 Douglas Dickins F.R.P.S.
188 Isaac Kehimkar/Porpoise Photostock
188 Sunjoy Monga/Porpoise Photostock

The boundary of India as depicted here and in other maps of this book is neither authentic nor correct.